# Bedtime

# *Blessings*

### 100 Bedtime Stories & Activities
for Blessing Your Child

# Bedtime Blessings

100 Bedtime Stories & Activities
for Blessing Your Child

## by
## JOHN TRENT, Ph.D.

Tyndale House Publishers, Wheaton, Illinois

Heritage Builders

BEDTIME BLESSINGS

Copyright © 2000 by John Trent
All rights reserved. International copyright secured.

ISBN: 1-56179-797-9

A Focus on the Family book published by Tyndale House Publishers,
Wheaton, Illinois.

Editor: Jane Vogel
Cover design: Steve Diggs & Friends, Nashville, TN
Illustrations: Arden von Haeger

Printed in the United States of America

00 01 02 03 04 05 06/10 9 8 7 6 5 4 3 2 1

# Table of Contents

# Introduction

As far back as Old Testament times, parents were giving a blessing to their children, and those children longed to receive it. (Read Genesis 27 and the story of Jacob and Esau to see the immense joy of receiving a parent's blessing, and the heartbroken sobs from one who missed it.) This collection of bedtime blessings is designed to create special moments between you and your child, something like a goodnight kiss before turning out the light. It is a mix of stories, activities, and games, each ending with a short prayer you can pray aloud before tucking your child in bed.

These prayers are purposely short for little attention spans. But feel free to make up your own prayer, to make the prayers longer, or to have your child pray along with you. Whatever you do, be sure to personalize the prayer as suggested in each one, by using your child's name and perhaps including something you and your child talked about during the story or activity.

Your prayer can become a little blessing ceremony, giving you the chance to affirm your child in a special way. Try one or more of these ideas to set off the prayer time:

- Just before you pray, say something like, "It's time for your blessing prayer!" That can help set apart your prayer time as one when you lift your child before the Heavenly Father for His blessing. Watch how quickly your child will pick up on your setting apart this time. Soon you'll be able to ask, "What time is it?" when you finish the story or activity, and your child will respond, "It's time for my blessing prayer!" Having your child ask for a blessing prayer warms your heart as well as your child's.

• Don't forget the power of meaningful touch. Praying as you hold hands or hug your child is a wonderful way to grow even closer and send him or her off to sleep.

• Consider concluding your prayer with a blessing straight from God's Word. Numbers 6:24 offers a beautiful blessing that you can personalize for your child: "May the Lord bless you and take good care of you. May the Lord smile on you and be gracious to you. May the Lord look on you with favor, _____ *[your child's name]*, and give you His peace." Children like to listen to things over and over (have you noticed how they'll play a song or tape again and again?). Hearing God's Word applied to their lives for 100 nights can be a special blessing in and of itself!

Some of the blessing activities and prayers in this book are designed to show that you care about the details of your child's life, with your concern being reinforced by *meaningful touch*. Others are designed to communicate a *spoken message* of love. Still others include words that help them see their *high value* to God and to you. Still others show the *special future* and *genuine commitment* you and the Lord have for your child.

Let's look at each of those blessing ingredients.

*Meaningful touch.* You can communicate affirmation without saying a word. Meaningful touch could include having your child sit right next to you when you read the blessing, playing with your child's hair, holding hands when you pray, hugging your child before you tuck him or her into bed. All these small things communicate your blessing.

*Spoken words.* Biblically, a blessing was given when it was spoken. Your words—when you are speaking your child's name, reading together, saying, "I love you," and praying for your child—can etch a deep sense of being loved into your child's memory.

*Attaching high value.* The word for *blessing* in the Scriptures means to "bow the knee." We bow before someone who is very valuable. When we bless the Lord, we're saying, "Lord, You're so valuable, I bow my heart before You." When we bless our children, we're attaching high value to them through our words, appropriate touch, and genuine commitment.

*Special future.* When children hear words from a parent, grandparent, or other loved one that picture a special future for them, they rise to those words. Helping your children see that God has a special future for them

(Jeremiah 29:11), and that you appreciate their unique character traits and talents, can fill up their hearts with your blessing.

*Genuine commitment.* In a world full of insecurity, knowing that a loving parent or grandparent will be there for them gives children a tangible sense of stability. Helping children understand that their Heavenly Father will always be there for them builds their lives on the Rock.

Meaningful touch, spoken words, attaching high value, picturing a special future, and genuine commitment*— those five elements of this powerful, biblical tool are stitched together in the blessings that follow. Over the course of 100 evenings, you'll create a quilt of memories—memories of moments when you talked together, laughed together, played together, and prayed together.

They'll be memories that can provide warmth and comfort for a lifetime—for both of you.

John Trent, Ph.D.
President, Encouraging Words and
Strongfamilies.com

* If you'd like to look more closely at the biblical practice of blessing children and how it can shape young lives, please see *Pictures the Heart Remembers* (John Trent, WaterBrook Press) and *The Gift of the Blessing* (Gary Smalley and John Trent, Thomas Nelson Publishers).

# The Blessings Box

Some of the blessings that follow require certain materi-
als—mostly easy-to-find household items. These are listed
at the start of each activity so you can gather them ahead
of time. A complete list of all the supplies is provided
here. If you wish, gather the supplies in a "blessings box"
so you'll have them ready whenever you need them.

index cards
blunt scissors
pencils
the cartoon section of your newspaper—a Sunday
    section, if possible
black-and-white cartoon page from your newspaper
plastic drinking straws
plastic cup
bubble mix with a bubble ring or wand
flashlight
construction paper
photo of yourself as a child
package of bean seeds
small flowerpot or cup
potting soil
magnifying glass
stationery
envelope
postage stamp
paring knife
crayons

four toothpicks
childhood toys of yours, if you have them
cardboard tube from a roll of paper towels
empty soda bottle
nut in its shell—the kind you can easily open
    (or a small treat in a box)
deck of cards ("Old Maid," "Go Fish," etc.)
charcoal briquettes (not the self-starting kind)
¼ cup of salt
¼ cup of laundry bluing
1 tablespoon of ammonia
disposable pie pan
one die
paper
pepper
liquid soap
apple
slice of lemon
flower
two fat rubber bands
bottle cap
checker board
two kinds of food to use as checkers (small cookies, crackers,
    candies, fruit, or vegetables)
tissues
waxed paper
watch with a second hand
adhesive bandages
popped popcorn

LET'S PLAY A GAME
# Fat Cat

Tonight's game is "Fat Cat." Fat Cats are word pairs that rhyme, like "fat cat" or "funny bunny."

Here's how you play. One person thinks of a Fat Cat, and then gives a clue so the other person can guess what it is. For example, the clue I might give for "funny bunny" could be "laughable rabbit." For "fat cat," I could say, "chubby kitty."

I'll start.

*[Here are a few to get you started: rude dude; old cold; tan man; dragon wagon; snake cake; silly lily; ants' pants. When you and your child have each had a few turns and you're ready to quit, close with the appropriate choice from the following pairs, which translate "fun son" and "pearl girl."]*

I have one last Fat Cat, and it's about you! You are an "enjoyable boy"/"jewel daughter."

Dear Father in heaven,
Thank You for all the fun You give us. And thank You for a "fun son"/"pearl girl" like _____ *[your child's name]* to share it with.
     Amen.

## LET'S TALK ABOUT FEELINGS
# Feeling Sad

There's a little book called *Misery* by Suzanne Heller (Paul S. Eriksson, 1967) that tells about some of the very sad things that sometimes happen to us. *Misery* is another word for *sadness*. Here are a few of the miserable things the book lists:

"Misery is when you've told your best friend personal things and you find out she's not your best friend anymore."

"Misery is when you've got your birthday and the measles on the same day."

"Misery is when your baby sister goes into *your* room and eats *your* finger paints and *you* get the blame."

The last entry in the book reads, "Misery is when grownups don't realize how miserable kids can feel."

I don't want to be a grownup who doesn't understand when you feel miserable. I want to know what makes you miserable and sad. Can you think of some of them? I'll start the sentence, and you finish it.

I feel sad when _____.

I feel sad when _____.

I feel sad when _____.

Did you know that God cares about what makes you sad, too? Let's talk to God about that.

Dear God,
Thank You that You care when _____ *[your child's name]* is sad, or lonely, or tired, or upset. Thank You, too, for my precious _____ *[your child's name].* When things like _____
happen *[list here the things your child mentioned that make him or her sad],* You still care for him/her, Lord, and so do I.

    Amen.

LET'S TALK ABOUT THE FUTURE
# When I Grow Up

Let's pretend you're grown up—say, my age. What kind of person would you like to be? Do you want to be ...

- Someone who frowns a lot *[make a mad face]* or smiles a lot *[smile at your child]*?

- Someone who is kind to animals *[pretend to pet an animal]* or who makes animals run away and hide *[make scared yipping-type noises]*?

- Someone who is kind to others *[hand your child a teddy bear, pillow, or other handy object]* or someone who is selfish *[grab the object back]*?

- Someone who praises God *[fold your hands or raise them in an attitude of praise]* or who praises only him/herself *[pantomime a proud attitude by pointing your thumb to your chest, posing like a muscle-man, or something similar]*?

What else do you want to be like?

*[Allow your child time for open-ended response.]*

How do you think you can grow up to be that kind of person?

*[Affirm any ideas your child suggests, like being kind to others now, sharing toys with a sibling, going to church or Sunday school.]*

One very important way to grow up to be a good and kind grown-up is to ask God to help you. Let's do that right now.

Dear God,
Please help this special child of mine to grow up to be kind, and cheerful, and loving, and _____
*[list any additional responses your child made]*. Especially help _____ *[your child's name]* to love and praise You.
     Amen.

LET'S TALK ABOUT THE DAY
# Good Day/Bad Day

*[Before you begin this blessing, decide on a form of meaningful touch that you can give to your child and then your child can give to you. Some ideas include:*

- *Lightly brush your fingertips up and down your child's arm;*

- *Rub your child's back or shoulders;*

- *Smooth your child's hair.]*

Let's talk about each other's day. While you talk, I'll lightly brush my fingertips up and down your arm *[or whatever form of touch you've chosen]*. When you're finished, I'll tell you about my day, and you can brush your fingertips up and down my arm.

So tell me. How was your day? Was it a good day, a bad day, or just an okay day?

*[Talk about your child's response. What made the day good (or bad or okay)? What was the best part? What does your child hope will go better tomorrow?]*

Now I'll tell you about my day.

*[Share some of the highlights of your day with your child. Don't be afraid to share some of your challenges and how you faced them, as long as you don't burden your child with adult problems.]*

Do you know who else we can share our day with? We can share it with God. He already knows what was bad and good, but He's glad when we tell Him about it in our prayers, too.

Dear God,
Thank You for the good things that happened today.
Thank You for _____ *[name some of the positive things your child and you mentioned]*.
Thank You for helping us get through the not-so-good things that happened today, like _____
*[name some of the negative events you and your child mentioned]*. Please give _____ *[your child's name]*
a really great day tomorrow!
    Amen.

LET'S SING A SONG
# Jesus Loves Me

Let's sing a song together!

> Jesus loves me, this I know,
> For the Bible tells me so.
> Little ones to Him belong.
> They are weak but He is strong.
> Yes, Jesus loves me.
> Yes, Jesus loves me.
> Yes, Jesus loves me.
> The Bible tells me so.

Do you like that song? Why?

Jesus loves all people, but especially He loves children. Why do you think that is?

There is an interesting passage in the Bible that tells how dear you are to Him. Let me read it to you. It's found in Matthew 18:1-5.

At that time the disciples came to Jesus. They asked him, "Who is the most important person in the kingdom of heaven?"

Jesus called a little child over to him. He had the child stand among them. Jesus said, "What I'm about to tell you is true. You need to change and become like little

children. If you don't you will never enter the kingdom of heaven. Anyone who becomes as free of pride as this child is the most important in the kingdom of heaven.

"Anyone who welcomes a little child like this in my name welcomes me."

Let's thank Jesus for how much He loves you.

Dear Jesus,
Thank you for how much You love _____
*[your child's name]*. And thank You for giving us the Bible that tells us so.
     Amen.

## LET'S DO AN EXPERIMENT
# Step Through a Card

*[You will need a few index cards and a pair of blunt scissors.]*

This is going to seem impossible, but it's not. I want you to take this index card and cut a hole in it big enough for you to put your foot through.

*[Give your child the scissors and a couple of index cards. Let him or her try to cut a big enough hole.]*

Give up? Let me show you how.

*[Fold the card in the middle. Cut out a notch as the illustration indicates. Then make seven or nine cuts, alternating with one cut starting at the fold and the other starting at the edge of the card. When you're finished, unfold the card and have your child step through it.]*

This job seemed impossible at first, but it really wasn't, was it? Did you know that the Bible says, "With God all things are possible" (Matthew 19:26)? That doesn't just mean that God knows special tricks with scissors, the way I solved this problem. It means that God is big enough and strong enough to solve any problem.

Can you think of something you have to do that seems really hard—maybe even impossible?

*[Guide your child away from riddles like, "Can God make two mountains with no valley in between?" Help him or her instead to think of something practical in everyday life, such as getting along with a sibling all day without fighting, or mastering a particular challenge at school.]*

Let's ask God to help make that job possible for you.

Dear God,
Please help _____ *[your child's name]* with
_____ *[the "impossible" task*
*your child mentioned]*. Thank You that it is not impossible for You, even though it seems impossible to
_____ *[your child's name]*.
   Amen.

JUST A REMINDER . . .

### Meaningful Touch

You can communicate your blessing without saying a word. Meaningful touch could include having your child sit right next to you when you read the blessing, playing with your child's hair, holding hands when you pray, hugging your child before you tuck him or her into bed. All these small things communicate your blessing.

LET'S PLAY A GAME

# Tongue Twisters

Tonight's game is Tongue Twisters. I'll read a tongue twister. Then you see if you can say it three times— really fast—without tripping up. When you've had a turn, I'll try.

• Toy boat

• She sells sea shells by the seashore

• Truly rural

• Lemon liniment

• Red leather, yellow leather

• How much wood would a woodchuck chuck if a woodchuck could chuck wood?

Let's thank God for making our tongues and for giving us funny things to do together.

Dear God,
Thank You for the fun _____ *[your child's name]* and I have together. Thank You for giving us tongues to talk with and laugh with and pray with.
　　　　　Amen.

## LET'S WRITE A LETTER TO GOD
# Getting in Trouble

*[You will need a pencil.]*

Here's a letter from a six-year-old.

Dear Lord,
Do You love everybody? Even little boys who get into a lot of trubble?
        Mark*

What do you think? Does God love children even if they get into trouble?

Do you think He listens to our prayers when we're in trouble?

Now let's write a letter to God from you. We'll use the space across the page.

*[If your child doesn't know how to write, have your child dictate a letter. When you're finished, let your child draw a picture on the page.]*

Dear God,
Thank You that You hear our prayers, even when we're in trouble. Please listen to _____'s *[your child's name]* prayer. *[Read the letter your child wrote or dictated.]*
        Amen.

*From *Dear Lord*, selected by Bill Adler (Thomas Nelson, 1982).

# Bedtime Blessings

LET'S HEAR A STORY
# Me-First Mouse

Once four mice lived in a hole in the kitchen wall. Their names were Me, Pete, Repeat, and Repeat-after-me.

One night they got thirsty and looked from their hole to see a saucer.

"Milk!" they said.

Me pushed to the front. "Me first."

"Why should *you* go first?" said Pete.

"I've got the shortest name, that's why," the mouse said, tiptoeing out.

"Then I should be second," said Pete. "My name's next to shortest."

"*I* should be second," said Repeat-after-me. "After all, I'm '*after me.*'"

"No," said Repeat. "I'm Repeat, and Repeat should go after Me."

They got into such an argument it woke the cat. And guess what happened to Me?

*[Let your child answer, then talk about the following questions.]*

Do you ever have a hard time letting other people go first?

When do you most want to say, "Me first"?

*[If your child has trouble thinking of situations, mention those you've observed as difficult for him or her— maybe waiting for a turn on the playground slide or at a drinking fountain, being served dessert, or opening presents at a family gathering.]*

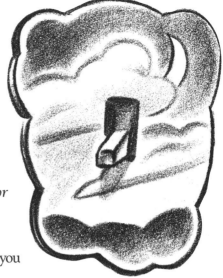

Let's ask God to help you when it's hard to wait your turn.

Dear God,
Help _____ *[your child's name]* not to say, "Me first," or push ahead in line, even _____ *[list the situations your child mentioned]*. Thank You for the times when _____ *[your child's name]* does get to be first, and thank You for the times when he/she waits patiently for his/her turn.

      Amen.

LET'S READ THE FUNNIES
# Favorite Funnies

*[You will need the cartoon section of your newspaper. Get a Sunday one, if possible, since it is in color.]*

*[This is a really simple way to spend time together. Simply open the "funny papers" on the bed and let your child pick the ones he or she would like you to read. When you're finished, you might ask which one your child liked best and why.]*

If there were a comic strip about you, what might it be like? Would you be a superhero, a kid who says funny things, or what?

How would you want the artist to draw you?

Could I be in your comic strip? How would you want the artist to draw me?

Dear God,
Thank You for the times when _____ *[your child's name]* and I can just be together like this. Thank You for funny papers and for the gift of laughter. Thank You for giving _____ *[your child's name]* and me each other to love. We love You, too.
        Amen.

LET'S TALK ABOUT WHEN I WAS YOUR AGE
# Parent Picture

*[You will need a photo of yourself as a child.]*

*[Show your child the photo.]*

Who do you think that is?

It's me.

*[Describe yourself at the time of the photo: your age, your house, your bedroom, what you thought about at night, what you prayed about if you prayed.]*

Is there anything you would like to ask that child?

I think if the two of us had grown up together, we would have been good friends. What do you think?

Even though I'm a grown-up, there's still a part of me that's a little child. I still like to play and hear stories. And I still like to be with little children. Especially with you.

Dear God,
Thank You for this dear child You've given me. Help us, as we grow older, always to be great friends. In Jesus' name we pray.
      Amen.

## LET'S DO A PUZZLE
# Puppy Puzzle

*[You will need a pencil and an eraser.]*

Pretend that a few months ago your dog gave birth to nine puppies. For a while they all played together and got along just fine. But now they all fight so much that you have to do something to separate them. You have them all in the one kennel shown across the page. You have to separate these nine dogs into their own individual pens by drawing two squares.

Use a pencil to draw two squares on the opposite page. You can erase your squares and try again if you don't make nine separate pens on your first try.

If you want a hint, look at the bottom of this page.

If you want the answer, look at the back of the book.

*[If your child gets frustrated, draw the angled square as shown in the back of the book. Then ask your child if he or she can add one square to solve the puzzle.]*

Hint: One square will be small, and one square will be standing on its corner like a diamond.

Dear God,
Thank You for puzzles to solve and for clues to help us solve them. Thank You for teamwork when we have hard puzzles. Thank You that _____ *[your child's name]* and I can work together on this puzzle and that we can be together in our family.

  Amen.

### LET'S DO AN EXPERIMENT
## Blowing Bubbles

*[You will need a plastic straw, a plastic cup, bubble mix, and a bubble ring or wand.]*

Let's blow bubbles.

*[Take a few minutes to let your child play with the bubbles.]*

Now let's try an experiment. Let's see if we can blow a bubble inside another one. Do you think we can do it?

*[Turn the plastic cup upside down and wet it. Then dip the bubble ring in the soapy mix, blow a large bubble, and*

*carefully place it on the bottom of the plastic cup. Next, wet the plastic straw in the soapy mix and slowly push it inside the larger bubble. Gently blow a smaller bubble inside the larger one, making sure you don't touch the wet wall of the larger bubble with the smaller one.]*

What do you think of our bubble-inside-a-bubble? Amazing, isn't it? Do you want to know something even more amazing? When you belong to Jesus, Jesus lives inside of you! He lives in your heart! Now, that's amazing!

*[If you wish, you can ask your child if he or she knows that Jesus lives in his or her heart. You may wish to invite your child to ask Jesus into his or heart, if you feel that's an appropriate step right now. You can guide your child in a simple prayer like this: "Dear Jesus, I love You and want to live for You. Please forgive me for the things I've done wrong. Please live inside my heart." Whether or not you pray this prayer with your child, conclude your time together with a blessing prayer like the one below.]*

Dear Jesus,
Thank You that You love _____ *[your child's name]* so much that You want to live in his/her heart. Please keep filling up _____
*[your child's name]* with Your love.
      Amen.

### LET'S LOOK IN THE BIBLE
# The Lord Is My Shepherd

*[You will need a Bible.]*

*[Sometimes we need to give children a chance to respond to God's Word without a lot of direct teaching from us. This activity does just that.]*

What do you know about shepherds? What do you think they do for the sheep they take care of?

When the sheep are tired, what do you think the shepherd does?

When the sheep are thirsty, what do you think the shepherd does?

When the sheep get lost, what do you think the shepherd does?

Did you know that the Bible says that God is our shepherd? Listen.

*[Read Psalm 23:1-3.]*

Did you ever think of yourself as a little lamb that belongs to God?

How do you think the Lord is like your shepherd?

How do you think you are like one of God's sheep?

Let's talk to God about being His sheep.

Dear God,
Thank You that _____ *[your child's name]* is Your little lamb, and that You take care of him/her like a shepherd. Thank You that You _____ *[name some of the ways your child said the Lord was like a shepherd]*. Thank You that You love us. We love You.
      Amen.

LET'S LOOK AT NATURE
# Night Sky

*[Use this blessing on a clear night. Turn out the lights and look out the window with your child, talking quietly about what you see in the sky. Use questions like the following to let your child tell you about what he or she sees.]*

Can you see the moon tonight?

How many stars can you see?

Did you know that God made more stars than we can even count? Some are so far away that we can't even see them all.

The Bible tells us that the skies show us what God has made.* What can you see in the sky that God made?

Sometimes people like to make a wish when they see the first star in the night sky. But it would be even better to say a prayer to God, thanking Him for the things He's made. We can even pray with our eyes open for this prayer. Why don't you look out at the sky and thank God for the things you can see? Then I'll say a prayer with my eyes open.

*[After your child has prayed, turn his or her face to yours. Looking directly at your child, offer a blessing prayer like the one that follows.]*

* Psalm 19:1-2

Dear God,
Thank You for making the moon and the stars. And
thank You for making _____ *[your child's*
*name]*. Thank You that the stars are bright and beautiful,
and thank You that _____ *[your child's*
*name]* is _____ *[list two positive qualities*
*about your child, such as "loving," "kind," "cheerful"].*
    Amen.

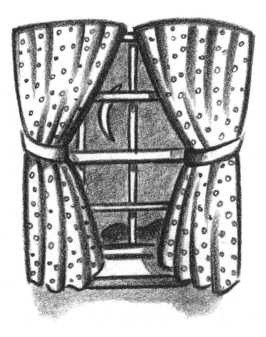

## LET'S DO AN EXPERIMENT
# Bean Seeds

*[You will need a package of bean seeds, a small flowerpot or cup filled with potting soil, and water.]*

*[Show your child the seed packet.]*

Do you know what's in this package?

*[Open the packet and shake a few seeds into your child's hand.]*

These are bean seeds. What do you think will happen if we plant them?

What do you think will grow from bean seeds?

Let's plant some seeds.

*[Help your child press several bean seeds into the potting soil. Be sure to use more than one seed so that you're more likely to get a plant. Add a little water to the pot.]*

How long do you think it will take for our bean seeds to grow?

Let's check the package and see what it says.

*[Read the germination time given on the package to your child.]*

Does that seem like a long time to wait?

Did you know that Jesus said God's Word is like a seed planted in our hearts? Once Jesus told a story about a farmer who planted seeds—just as we planted these bean seeds. Then Jesus explained His story. He said, "Here is what the story means. The seed is God's message....The seed on good soil stands for those with an honest and good heart. They hear the message. They keep it in their hearts. They remain faithful and produce a good crop" (Luke 8:11, 15).

When you listen to God's message in the Bible, and especially when you learn it by heart, you are planting a seed in your heart! You may not notice any difference right away, just as we don't see any bean plants growing from our bean seeds right away. But when you plant God's Word in your heart, eventually you will see a difference in your life.

Let's ask God to make our hearts like good garden soil, so that we will listen to His Word and keep it in our hearts.

Dear God,
Thank You that You give us Your Word in the Bible. Please plant Your Word in _____'s *[your child's name]* heart and in my heart. Help us to grow more and more like Jesus.
        Amen.

*[When your bean seeds begin to sprout, you may want to use one of the "Let's Plant a Seed" blessings. They're on pages 36, 82, 112, 118, 139, 156, and 176.]*

### LET'S PLANT A SEED
# Obey Your Parents

*[If you planted bean seeds (page 34), look at the plants that are growing. If you didn't plant seeds, use any growing plant for this activity.]*

*[Show your child the plant.]*

What's under the dirt in this pot?

*[Affirm whatever accurate answers your child gives— roots, water, etc.—but focus especially on the fact that a seed is in the dirt.]*

How do you know that there's a bean *[or whatever kind of plant you have]* seed in the dirt?

Even if you hadn't planted the seed yourself, you could tell that there's a bean seed in this pot— because you can see a bean plant!

Jesus tells us that God's Word is like a seed planted in our hearts. Let's plant one of those seeds in your heart tonight.

"Children, obey your parents in the Lord, for this is right" (Ephesians 6:1, NIV).

*[Read verse and have your child repeat it.]*

Remember that we can tell a bean seed is planted when we see a bean plant growing? How do you think we'll be able to tell that a verse about obeying your parents is planted in your heart?

*[Let your child respond.]*

When people see you obeying your parents, they will know that you have this verse planted in your heart! The verse is like a seed, and obeying is like the plant.

Let's ask God to help this seed grow.

Dear God,
Tonight we planted a seed from Your Word in
_____'s *[your child's name]* heart. Help that
seed to grow. Help _____ *[your child's name]*
to obey me *[also name the child's other parent if appropriate]*. Thank You for all the ways _____ *[your child's name]* already obeys.
      Amen.

LET'S DO AN EXPERIMENT
# Magnificent Magnification

*[You will need a magnifying glass and a Bible.]*

Let's go exploring—right here on your bed.

*[Give your child the magnifying glass.]*

Look at your arm. What do you see that you didn't notice before?

Now look at my arm.

Now what do you want to look at? How about my eye? What do you see?

Let's look at a verse in the Bible.

*[Turn to Hebrews 4:13 and let your child look at it with the magnifying glass. Then read the verse aloud.]*

Do you think God's eyes are stronger than this magnifying glass?

Do you think God can see all the way to what's inside of us—even in our hearts?

*[Turn to 1 Samuel 16:7 and let your child look at it with the magnifying glass. Then read the verse aloud.]*

What do you think God sees when He looks at us? Can He see our thoughts?

*[Turn to Psalm 139:1-4 and let your child look at it with the magnifying glass. Then read the verse aloud.]*

What do you think God sees when He looks at your heart? What thoughts does He see when He looks at what you're thinking?

What do you hope God will notice when He looks at your heart and your thoughts?

Dear God,
It's amazing that You see everything inside us, even what we think and feel. Thank You that You love us even when our thoughts or our feelings aren't very nice. Thank You that You love _____ ____ *[your child's name]* even when _____ __ *[name some of the negative thoughts or feelings your child mentioned].* Thank You that You notice when _____ *[your child's name]* is feeling _____ *[name the things your child wants God to notice].* Help me to notice those things, too.

  Amen.

LET'S WRITE A SONG
# Sing a New Song

*[You will need a pencil.]*

"Praise the Lord. Sing a new song to the Lord" (Psalm 149:1a).

Let's write a "new song" to the Lord. You think of what you want to praise Him for, and I'll write it down. Here are some ideas to get you started:

- Names of family members;

- Fun things you like to do;

- Food you like to eat;

- Names of friends.

*[Write your child's suggestions in the blanks on the opposite page. If you can match the number of syllables to the number of blanks, your song will have the same meter as "Jesus Loves Me." But if you can't make it match up, it will still be a new song worth singing! When you've filled in the blanks, sing the song to the tune of "Jesus Loves Me." If your child is full of ideas, you can use the same format to write several stanzas. When you're done singing together, pray the following blessing prayer.]*

"I Praise Jesus"
[Sung to the tune of "Jesus Loves Me"]

I praise Jesus with my song,

for \_\_\_\_\_ \_\_\_\_\_ \_\_\_\_\_ \_\_\_\_\_ \_\_\_\_\_ \_\_\_\_\_.

I could praise Him all night long

for \_\_\_\_\_ \_\_\_\_\_ \_\_\_\_\_ \_\_\_\_\_ \_\_\_\_\_ \_\_\_\_\_.

Yes, I praise Jesus!

Yes, I praise Jesus!

Yes, I praise Jesus!

I praise Him with my song.


Dear God,
We praise You with this new song. We praise You for
_____ *[name the things your child offered
praise for in the song.]* We love You. And we love Your
Son Jesus. In His name we pray.
    Amen.

## LET'S TALK ABOUT THE FUTURE
# Future Family

Imagine that you are all grown up. Instead of living in this family, you have a new family of your own.

What kind of family would you like it to be?
If you get married, what kind of person would you like to marry?
If you have children, how many children would you like to have?
What kind of pets would you like in your family when you're a grown-up?
What will you have for dinner?
What rules would you have in your home?
What rules wouldn't you have?
It's never too early to start praying for your family. Let's start tonight!

Dear God,
A family is a wonderful thing. Thank You for ours.
Thank You for _____ [name each member of the family]. And thank You for the family that _____ [your child's name] will someday have. We pray they all love each other and take good care of each other.
Amen.

---

JUST A REMINDER . . .

### Spoken Words

Biblically, a blessing was never given until it was spoken. Your words—when you are speaking your child's name, reading together, saying, "I love you," and praying for your child—can etch a deep sense of being loved into your child's life.

## LET'S TALK ABOUT THE DAY
# Sundown Smoothing

Tell me about your day.

Did anything happen today that hurt your feelings or made you angry? While you tell me about it, let's imagine that I can smooth away all the bad feelings.

*[As your child talks, gently rub his or her hand, arm, back, or forehead.]*

Did you know that grown-ups sometimes get mad or have hurt feelings? Let me tell you about my day and you can smooth away my bad feelings.

God cares about our bad feelings. He even knows that it can be hard to get to sleep when we're feeling angry or hurt. This is what He tells us in the Bible:

"Do not let the sun go down while you are still angry" (Ephesians 4:26b).

Trying to smooth away the bad feelings can sometimes help you feel better.

*[Gently rub your child's hand, arm, back, or forehead again.]*

But sometimes you can get so angry that only God can help you get rid of the bad feelings.

Why don't we pray about those things that made you feel angry and hurt today?

Dear Father,
You know how bad _____ *[your child's name]* felt today when _____ *[name the situations your child mentioned]*. We give You all those hurt and angry feelings and ask You to take _____'s *[your child's name]* hurt and anger away. If he/she needs to forgive anyone, help him/her to do that. And help him/her to go to sleep tonight with all the bad feelings smoothed away.

   Amen.

### LET'S SING A SONG
# Jesus Loves the Little Children

Let's sing a song together!

>Jesus loves the little children,
>All the children of the world.
>Red, brown, yellow, black, and white,
>They are precious in His sight.
>Jesus loves the little children of the world.

Why do you think Jesus loves children?
How much do you think He loves them?
Does it make any difference what color they are?
What language they speak?
Where they live?
How much do you think He loves you?
Does He ever stop loving you?
How about when you're disobedient or when you're
    grumpy?
Let's pray to Jesus about His love.

Dear Jesus,
Thank You for loving all the children of the world, no
matter where they live, and no matter what they look
like or talk like. Especially I thank You for loving this
child of mine. I love him/her, too.

>Amen.

LET'S PLAY A GAME
# Twenty Questions

Tonight's game is Twenty Questions. We're going to play it in a special way that reminds us of how much we love each other.

I'll think of something in this room that could remind me of how much I love you. Maybe I'll pick your pillow, because I love to see you sleeping when I come in to check on you before I go to bed. But I won't tell you what I'm thinking of.

You get to ask me up to 20 questions to figure out what I'm thinking of—but I have to be able to answer all your questions either "yes" or "no." For example, you could not ask, "How big is it?" but you could ask, "Is it bigger than my foot?"

*[After your child guesses your object, explain why it reminds you of how much you love him or her. Then let your child choose an object for you to guess. Go back and forth until you're ready to close the day with prayer.]*

Dear Father,
Thank You for guessing games. And thank You that we don't have to guess whether or not You love us —we know You do! Help _____ *[your child's name]* to know how much I love him/her.
    Amen.

## LET'S WRITE A LETTER TO SOMEONE YOU LOVE
# Thanks for You!

*(You will need a pencil, some stationery, an envelope, your address book, and a stamp.)*

Did you know that many of the books of the Bible were first written as letters? Here's part of a letter that Paul wrote to some Christians he knew:

"I thank my God every time I remember you" (Philippians 1:3).

I think Paul must really have loved those Christians to write that to them, don't you?

Let's write a letter tonight to someone you love. Who would that be?

What would you like to say in your letter?

*[Help your child if he or she doesn't know how to write. You could include a recent photo of your child or a picture your child has drawn. Then look up the address and have your child put a stamp on the envelope.]*

Remember what Paul wrote in his letter, that he thanked God for the people he was writing to? What can you think of to thank God for about _____
*[the person to whom your child wrote]*?

Let's write "Philippians 1:3" on the back of the envelope, kind of like a secret code! When _____ *[the person to whom your child wrote]* looks it up, he/she will know that we were thinking of things to thank God for.

Let's thank God for

_____

*[the person to whom your child wrote]* right now.

Dear God,
Thank You for _____ *[the person to whom your child wrote]*. Thank You for _____ *[list some of the things your child mentioned about the person]*. Please bless _____ *[the person to whom your child wrote]*. And please bless _____ *[your child's name]*.
　　　Amen.

LET'S HEAR A STORY
# Jungle Journey—Part 1

This is a story about a boy who didn't give a hoot about advice.

A boy once ran a cross-country route through a dangerous jungle. At the beginning of his journey, a group of owls greeted him.

"The jungle is a dangerous place," said one owl.

"I know," the boy replied.

"You will need directions and help from those who can see the land from the air," offered another owl.

"I'll be okay. I can take care of myself," the boy insisted.

"Many who enter the jungle never find their way out," warned the other owl.

"Don't have time to sit around and talk. Gotta go." With that, the boy was off and running. The owls looked at each other and shook their heads.

Unfortunately, the boy got lost.

. . . And we'll have to wait until tomorrow night to find out what happened next!

What do you think will happen to the boy?

If you were in the jungle, would you listen to the owls?

How do you usually feel when I tell you how I think you should do something?

*[Give a few examples of the kind of direction you give your child—perhaps offering help or direction in tying shoes or choosing what clothes to wear.]*

How much are you like the boy in this story?

Let's pray about listening when people want to help us.

Dear God,
Help _____ *[your child's name]* listen when someone is trying to help, even if he/she thinks he/she can do it by him/herself. And help me to listen to _____ *[your child's name]* so I know when he/she doesn't need help.
          Amen.

### LET'S HEAR A STORY
# Jungle Journey—Part 2

This is the continuing story about a boy who didn't give a hoot about advice.

*[Go back to page 50 and read the story from the beginning.]*

. . . Fortunately, he was found.

Unfortunately, it was by a rhinoceros that chased him.

Fortunately, he climbed a palm tree and the rhino left.

Unfortunately, a group of monkeys was having a party at the top of the tree and began to throw coconuts at him.

Fortunately, he grabbed a nearby vine and swung away from the monkeys.

Unfortunately, the vine broke and he fell into the river.

Fortunately, the boy climbed onto a floating log.

Unfortunately, the log turned out to be an alligator.

. . . And we'll have to wait until tomorrow to find out what happened next!

What do you think will happen next?

What would you do if you were the boy?

What's the most dangerous thing that has happened to you?

Dear God,
Thank You for imagination and adventures! And thank You that _____ *[your child's name]* almost never has to climb a coconut tree to get away from a wild rhinoceros. Please take care of _____ *[your child's name]*, though, when he/she is in _____ *[name the dangerous situation your child mentioned]*. Thank You that You can help him/her to make smart choices and be safe.
     Amen.

LET'S HEAR A STORY
# Jungle Journey—Part 3

This is the continuing story about a boy who didn't give a hoot about advice.

*[Go back to page 50 and read the story from the beginning.]*

. . . Fortunately, the alligator swam ashore, leaving the boy to float down the river.

Unfortunately, the reason the alligator swam to shore was that they were drifting toward a waterfall.

Fortunately, it was a short waterfall.

Unfortunately, the pool the boy fell into was filled with man-eating fish that proceeded to bite him in the pants.

Fortunately, his pants were old and needed to be replaced anyway.

Unfortunately, his legs didn't.

Fortunately, the fish choked on his pants and never got to his legs, so the boy swam to shore.

Unfortunately, he ran right into a hippopotamus that was sunbathing.

Fortunately, the hippo yawned and the boy escaped.

Unfortunately, while running away, the boy fell into a pit dug by a trapper to catch hippos.

Fortunately, the boy heard footsteps and called for help.

Unfortunately, the footsteps belonged to the hippo, who was galloping toward the pit.

Fortunately, the boy looked up and saw the group of owls he had encountered at the beginning of his journey.

"Help me! I'll be crushed to death if the hippo falls into the pit!"

. . . And we'll pick up the story there tomorrow night!

What do you think will happen next?

What would you do if you were the boy?

When you're in trouble, who do you ask to help you?

Who are some other people who help you?

Dear God,
Thank You for giving _____ [your child's name] people like _____ [list the helpers your child identified] to help when _____ [your child's name] is in trouble. Thank You that You help him/her, too. And please keep teaching _____ [your child's name] to make good choices so he/she doesn't get into trouble.

Amen.

LET'S HEAR A STORY
# Jungle Journey—Part 4

This is the continuing story about a boy who didn't give a hoot about advice.

*[Go back to page 50 and read the story from the beginning.]*

. . . "If you would have asked for advice at the beginning of your journey, you would have never fallen into the pit in the first place," said one of the owls.

"Or fallen down the waterfall," said another.

"Or from the tree," said the other.

Meanwhile, the thumps of the hippo's feet grew louder.

"Please help me!" cried the boy. "I'll listen. I promise." The owls turned their heads slowly and looked at each other. They nodded, then turned to the boy and said, "Squeeze into the near corner of the pit. When the hippo falls, jump onto his back.

You will be high enough then to crawl out."

It was not exactly the type of advice the boy had hoped for, but it was the only advice he had to go on, so he followed it.

Suddenly, the hippo fell into the pit with a loud CRASH! The boy jumped onto his back and, with the owls' directions, he made it safely through the jungle.

What is the lesson you learned from the story?

Listen to this verse from the Bible: "Where there is no guidance, the people fall, but in an abundance of counselors, there is victory" (Proverbs 11:14, NASB). What do you think that verse means?

Who do you know that gives you good advice or directions?

Dear God,
Thank You for people who give good advice, like
_____ [name the people your child mentioned.] Help _____ [your child's name] to listen to those people. And help us all to listen to what You teach us in the Bible.
     Amen.

## LET'S DO AN EXPERIMENT
# Salt of the Earth

*[You will need a plate, an apple, a paring knife, and a slice of lemon.]*

*[As your child watches, cut the apple in half and place both pieces on a plate. Squeeze lemon juice on one half, but leave the other half alone.]*

While we wait to see what happens to our apple pieces, let's read something from the Bible.

Once Jesus told the people who followed Him, "You are the salt of the earth" (Matthew 5:13a).

Do you have any ideas about what Jesus meant?

You know what we use salt for—we put it on food because we like the taste. But in Bible times, when people didn't have refrigerators, they put salt on food to keep it from going bad.

Food isn't the only thing that can go bad. Sometimes things can go bad on the playground. Can you think of an example?

Sometimes things can go bad in families. Can you think of an example of that?

What other ways can you think of that things can go bad?

*[Look again at the apple halves.]*

What difference do you see between these two halves of the apple?

This half of the apple is going bad. It's getting spoiled. It reminds me of how things get spoiled when _____ *[list the "going bad" examples your child just gave].*

*[Point to the apple half that you treated with lemon juice.]*

Why do you think that this half isn't going bad?

The lemon juice is keeping this half of the apple from going bad. That's how people in Bible times used salt— to keep meat from going bad.

Now think again about what Jesus said: that Christians are the salt of the earth. How can Christians like you and me help stop things from going bad? Not things like meat or apples, but things that go bad on the playground or in families or somewhere else?

*[Talk through each of the situations your child gave as examples of things going bad, helping him/her think of ways a Christian could help prevent or solve the problems.]*

Can you think of a time when you helped stop things from going bad?

Let's ask God to help us be "the salt of the earth" that helps keep things from going bad.

Dear God,
Thank You that _____ *[your child's name]* really is the salt of the earth. Thank You for the times when he/she _____ *[name the positive actions your child has identified]*. Help _____ *[your child's name]* and me and our whole family to be the salt of the earth for You.
    Amen.

LET'S LOOK AT NATURE
# Fancy Flowers

*[You will need a flower.]*

What can you learn from this flower?

One day when Jesus was teaching, He taught by using flowers. He said, "Why do you worry about clothes? See how the wild flowers grow. They don't work or make clothing. But here is what I tell you. Not even Solomon [who was a very rich king] in all of his glory was dressed like one of those flowers. If that is how God dresses the wild grass, won't He dress you even better?" (Matthew 6:28-30)

Do you ever worry? What sorts of things do you worry about?

*[As your child responds, resist the temptation to "explain away" his or her worries!]*

Whenever you get worried, look at the flowers. What is God saying to you through them?

Dear God,
Thank You for flowers and the lesson they teach, the comforting lesson that You are going to take good care of us. Thank You that You promise to take care of _____ *[your child's name]* even when he/she is worried about _____ *[list some of the worries your child mentioned].*
  Amen.

LET'S DO A PUZZLE
# Squares, Squares Everywhere

Look at the box across the page. How many squares can you find?

*[Let your child take as much time as he or she wants to count the squares. Don't point out any squares that he or she didn't see yet.]*

Did you find 16 squares? Good start. But look again. Where's the 17th?

*[Trace the big square with your finger.]*

Can you find any more?

*[Help your child see the squares made up of other squares. The total number of squares is given in the back of the book.]*

I think you are a little bit like this square. Do you know how? Just as there are more squares in this picture than you noticed right away, there is also more to you than people notice right away. At first look, people may see just your hair color or your height or weight or age. But there's more to you than that, isn't there? God sees it. And I see it, too. I see _____

*[list some positive qualities you see in your child, such as kindness, a love for art, athletic ability, honesty].*

Sunshine is grace. It's a gift we haven't earned. Jesus said that God causes the sun to shine on everyone, both the good and the bad.

Rain is a form of grace, too.

Can you think of some specific gifts God has given *you*?

Of all the gifts God has given us, what do you think is the greatest?

John 3:16 tells us about a gift from God. Listen: "God loved the world so much that He gave His one and only Son."

What do you say when someone gives you a gift, especially a really, really wonderful gift like Jesus?

You say thanks, of course!

Let's do that now.

Dear God,
Thank You that You love _____ *[your child's name]* so much that You gave him/ her _____ *[list the gifts your child mentioned]*. You are so kind and so generous. Especially we thank You for giving us Jesus.
     Amen.

LET'S READ THE FUNNIES
# Coloring the Comics

*[You will need crayons and the black-and-white cartoon section of your newspaper.]*

*[Spread the comic page over the bed and put something flat under it so you and your child can color. Have your child pick out a cartoon for you to read. Read it, then let your child color it. At the same time, you color one, too. Children love it when you get down on their level and participate with them in their activities. As you color, start a conversation by using questions like the following.]*

What colors are you using?

Why did you choose that color for that picture?

If you were going to choose a color for a happy picture, what color would you choose?

What's your favorite color?

Dear God,
Thank You that You have given us the gift of colors.
Thank You for favorite colors like _____
*[name your child's favorite color]* and for happy colors
like _____ *[name the color your
child picked for a happy picture]*. Thank You that You
fill our days with color and with laughter and with
happiness.
    Amen.

### LET'S LOOK IN THE BIBLE
# Rainbow Colors

*[You will need a Bible.]*

Why do you think God made rainbows?

Let's look in the Bible.

*[Read Genesis 9:8-16 aloud, paraphrasing it as needed to help your child understand the story.]*

Now that you've heard that story, why do you think God made rainbows?

When we see a rainbow, we can remember that God will never change His mind about the promises He makes to us.

Do you know what colors are in a rainbow? Here's a simple way to remember not just the colors but the order that the colors are found in a rainbow. Think of the name ROY G. BIV. The letters stand for:

R - Red

O - Orange

Y - Yellow

G - Green

B - Blue

I - Indigo

V - Violet

Whenever you see a rainbow, if you look closely, you'll see all those colors in exactly that order. The colors and the order never change! And God will never change His mind about His promises or about loving us.

Dear God,
Thank You that You loved Noah, and that You love Your world, and that You love _____ [your child's name]. Thank You for promising never to destroy the whole world with a flood again. Thank You that You never change Your mind about Your promises.
  Amen.

### LET'S DO A PUZZLE
# Toothpick Teaser

*[You'll need four toothpicks.]*

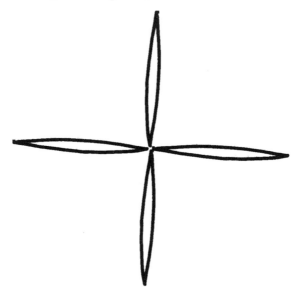

This puzzle is a tricky one! Let's see if we can make a square out of these toothpicks by moving only one of them.

*[If you get stumped, look at the bottom of page 72 for a clue. If you're really stumped, look in the back of the book for the answer.]*

Isn't it amazing that we could change the pattern with just one toothpick? You know, God can make big changes through just one person. Can you think of any people in the Bible whom God used to make big changes?

*[Help your child think of biblical characters like David when he fought Goliath, Moses leading the people out of Egypt, or Deborah leading Israel to victory.]*

Do you know anyone today who makes things better for the people around them?

*[Together talk about people you know who make a difference: teachers, people in your church, etc.]*

I see you as someone who makes a difference. You make a difference by _____ *[name some positive actions your child takes; for example, "when I'm sad, you can cheer me up with just a hug"; "when your best friend wants to play, you are the one person he/she really wants"].*

Let's talk to God about making a difference.

Dear God,
Just as one toothpick made a difference in this puzzle, one person can make a big difference, too. Thank You for people in the Bible, like _____ *[name the biblical characters you and your child talked about],*

who made a difference. Thank You for people we know, like _____ *[name the contemporary people you and your child talked about]*, who make a difference. Thank You that _____ *[your child's name]* can make a difference even though he/she is just _____ *[your child's age]* years old! Thank You that he/she already makes a difference by _____ *[list the positive actions you shared with your child]*.

    Amen.

(Hint: The square does not have to be a big one.)

Just a Reminder . . .

### Attaching High Value

The literal word for *blessing* in the Scriptures means to "bow the knee." We bow before someone who is very valuable. When we bless the Lord, we're saying, "Lord, You're so valuable, I bow my heart before You." When we bless our children, we're attaching high value to them through our words, appropriate touch, and genuine commitment.

LET'S BE THANKFUL
# Great Gifts

What is the best present you ever got?

*[Wait for your child's response.]*

Do you know what one of my best presents is?

*[Let your child guess.]*

Here's a hint from the Bible: "Children are a gift from the Lord" (Psalm 127:3a). Now can you guess what one of my best presents is?

You! You are one of the best presents I've ever gotten.

*[Take a few minutes to share with your child a story about how he or she joined your family—perhaps about the day he or she was born or was adopted.]*

When we get a really wonderful gift, what are we supposed to do?

*[If necessary, prompt your child until he or she remembers that we're supposed to say, "Thank you."]*

I want to do that now. I want to thank God for giving you to me. I'm going to talk to God now. You can listen.

Dear God,
Thank You *so* much for _____ *[your child's name]*. What a really, really wonderful gift You gave me when he/she joined our family. _____ *[your child's name]* is even a better present than _____ *[list the gifts your child mentioned as his/her favorites and those he/she guessed as your favorites]*. Thank You.
        Amen.

LET'S HAVE A RIDDLE
# Little Riddles

*[Here are some riddles that will be fun for the two of you to solve. If you get stumped, the answers are in the back of the book.]*

1. What is it that gets wetter the more it dries?

2. You throw a baseball as hard as you can. It doesn't hit anything and nothing is attached to it. Yet the ball comes right back to you. How can this be?

3. Jane lives on the tenth floor of an apartment building. She takes an elevator all the way down in the morning. When she returns in the afternoon, she takes the elevator to the seventh floor, gets off, and walks the rest of the way up the stairs to her apartment. Why does she have to do that?

Were these riddles hard or easy?

Do you think you'd like to ask one of your friends these riddles? Who would you like to ask?

Do you think your friend will guess the answers?

Suppose I asked you these riddles again. Would you get the answers this time?

Riddles seem pretty easy once you know the answers, don't they? Did you know that God knows the answers to all the riddles in the world? God knows everything there is to know! That's why God is never stumped or confused or mixed up. He knows everything!

Let's talk to Him now.

Dear God,
You know everything! We praise You for that! You know the answer to every riddle, and how many stars are in the sky, and how many hairs are on _____'s *[your child's name]* head. We're glad that You are in charge of the world and of our lives.
    Amen.

## LET'S TALK ABOUT WHEN I WAS YOUR AGE
# Favorite Toys

*[You will need some of your childhood toys, if you have them.]*

When I was little, these were some of my favorite toys.

*[Show your child the toys.]*

When I was young, one of my favorite things to do was

_____.

The reason I liked doing it so much was

_____.

Some of my friends then were

_____.

My best friend was

_____.

The reason that person was my best friend was

_____.

The neighborhood I grew up in was

_____.

My favorite thing about my neighborhood was

_____.

My favorite holiday was

_____.

The reason why it was my favorite holiday was

_____.

My favorite thing to do in the summer was

_____.

What have been some of *your* favorite memories?

Dear God,
Thank You for the good things we have to look back on, for the memories of favorite things, favorite people, favorite times. Thank You for _____ *[list the things your child shared]*. You have been really good to us, and we want You to know how much we appreciate it. We love You.

     Amen.

## LET'S DO AN EXPERIMENT
# Hole in a Hand

*[You will need a cardboard tube from a roll of paper towels. If you can't find one, you can roll an 8 1/2 x 11 inch piece of paper into a tube.]*

*[This experiment uses an optical illusion. You may want to try it yourself first to make sure you can help your child see the illusion.]*

Look at your hands. Are they good and solid?

Guess what: I'm going to help you find a hole right through the middle of your hand! Don't worry; it won't hurt a bit.

Listen carefully and do just what I tell you.

First, hold the tube up to your eye.

Keep both eyes open and look at _____.

*[Choose an object across the room for your child to focus on with both eyes.]*

Next, take the hand that isn't holding the tube, and use it to cover your eye. Keep looking at the _____ *[the object across the room].*

Now, let's slowly move the hand covering your eye along the tube. Keep looking at the _____ *[the object across the room].*

*[Guide your child to move his/her hand away from the eye, with the hand still open and with one side touching the side of the tube.]*

Tell me to stop when you see the hole in your hand!

*[When your child's hand is about halfway down the tube, it should appear to your child that there is a hole right through the palm!]*

Put the tube down and look at your hand again. Is there really a hole in it?

Did you know your eyes could play cool tricks like that?

Who do you think made our eyes to be able to do such fun stuff?

Let's thank God for our eyes.

Dear God,
Thank You for giving me and _____ *[your child's name]* eyes that work. Thank You that we can have fun with games with our eyes. Thank You that we can have fun with each other.
      Amen.

### LET'S PLANT A SEED
# Honor Your Father and Mother

*[If you planted bean seeds (page 34), look at the plants that are growing.]*

Let's plant another seed. Not a seed in a pot, but a seed in your heart. Do you remember that Jesus said God's Word is like a seed planted in your heart?

Here is a Bible verse to learn by heart:

"Honor your father and mother" (Ephesians 6:2).

*[Read verse and have your child repeat it.]*

This "seed" verse is special because it has a blessing with it. Listen to the rest of the verse: "That is the first commandment that has a promise. 'Then things will go well with you'" (Ephesians 6:2b-3a).

What do you think it means to "honor"?

*[Talk with your child, in language that he or she will understand,*

*about the attitude of respect that honoring a parent implies. Don't limit the definition to the action of obedience.]*

Do you think you can obey your parents but not be honoring them?

Let me show you a way you could be obeying but not really honoring me. You pretend that you are me. I'll pretend that I am you. Now you tell me to go to bed.

*[When your child tells you to go to bed, throw a fit and stomp off to bed.]*

Did I obey you?

Did I honor you?

*[Now reverse roles, letting the child act out a proper response.]*

Dear God,
Help _____ *[your child's name]* learn to honor me *[name your child's other parent if appropriate]* so that things will go well with _____ *[your child's name]*. Thank You for promising that blessing when _____ *[your child's name]* honors me/us.
        Amen.

### LET'S TALK ABOUT THE FUTURE
# Career Choices

*[You will need a Bible.]*

What kind of work would you like to be doing someday?

Why?

*[If your child can't think of anything, ask questions like these: "What kind of work does your dad do? Your mom? Our neighbor? Which of those sound most interesting to you?"]*

How do you feel when you imagine a future like that for yourself?

Did you know that sometimes God calls people to do certain work when they're still very young?

*[Read the story of God calling David from 1 Samuel 16:1, 7-12.]*

Maybe God won't call you to be a king, but whatever work He gives you to do will be important to Him.

Let's pray about that.

*[Place your hand on your child as you pray.]*

Dear God,
Please help _____ *[your child's name]* to grow up good and kind and a strong Christian. Give him/her work that pleases You, helps others, and brings _____ *[your child's name]* joy—whether he/she works as _____ *[name the career choice your child mentioned]* or as something else. In Jesus' name we pray.
        Amen.

### LET'S DO AN EXPERIMENT
# Water Trombone

*[You will need an empty soda bottle and a drinking straw.]*

*[Before you start tonight's experiment, fill the soda bottle about three-quarters full with water.]*

Tonight we will be making a water trombone.

*[Put the straw in the bottle and blow across the top of the straw. Then let your child take a turn.]*

A real trombone is also called a slide trombone because you change the tone by sliding part of the instrument up and down. We can do the same thing with our water trombone.

*[Hold the bottle in your hand and the straw in the other. Now move the bottle up and down as you are blowing across the straw. Then give the instrument to your child.]*

What happens to the sound when you lower the bottle?

*[The sound will get lower.]*

What do you think will happen when you lift the bottle?

*[Have your child predict what will happen, then test his or her prediction. Let your child experiment with some tunes before you say your prayers.]*

Dear God,
Thank You for music, and for the joy it brings to us. Help our lives to be like music to other people's ears so that we can bring a little joy to their lives, too. Thank You for the joy that _____ *[your child's name]* brings me.

    Amen.

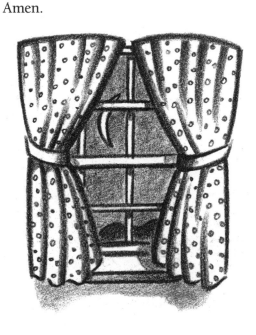

### LET'S TALK ABOUT THE DAY
# Encouragement/Discouragement

*[Before you begin this blessing, decide on a form of meaningful touch that you can give to your child and then your child can give to you. Some ideas include:*

- *Lightly brush your fingertips up and down your child's arm;*

- *Rub your child's back or shoulders;*

- *Smooth your child's hair.]*

Let's talk about each other's day. While you talk, I'll lightly brush my fingertips up and down your arm *[or whatever form of touch you've chosen]*. When you're finished, I'll tell you about my day, and you can brush your fingertips up and down my arm.

So tell me: How was your day? What was the most encouraging thing—something that made you feel good about yourself—that happened to you today? Why?

What was the most discouraging thing—something that made you feel not-so-good about yourself? Why?

*[Now trade roles and have your child ask questions.]*

Let's pray about those things.

Dear God,
Thank You for today. Thank You that _____
*[your child's name]* was encouraged by _____
*[name the encouraging things your child mentioned]*.
Help him/her not to be too discouraged about
_____ *[name the discouraging things
your child mentioned]*. Thank You that tomorrow is a
new day.
   Amen.

LET'S SING A SONG
# Swing Low, Sweet Chariot

*[Enjoy the hand motions to this song with your child.]*

Swing *[swing your arms]* low *[crouch]*,
Sweet *[kiss your fingertips]* chariot
*[shake the reins of the chariot]*,
Coming *[motion "come here" with your hands]* for
*[hold up four fingers]* to *[hold up two fingers]* carry
*[cradle your arms]* me *[point to yourself]* home
*[make the roof of a home with your hands]*.
Swing low *[repeat hand motions]*,
Sweet chariot *[repeat hand motions]*,
Coming for to carry me home *[repeat hand motions]*.

I *[point to your eye]* looked *[hold a flat hand over your
eyebrows as if looking]*
over Jordan, *[make a wavy motion with your hand to
simulate a river]*
and what *[put hand on cheek as if you're thinking]*
did I *[point to your eye]* see *[hold a flat hand over
your eyebrows as if looking]*,

Coming for to carry me home [repeat hand motions]?
A band [make the motion of a trombone playing] of angels
[flap your arms]
coming [motion "come here" with your hands]
after me [point to yourself].
Coming for to carry me home [repeat hand motions].
[Repeat chorus.]

[When you've finished, try it again, going faster, then faster still.]

Do you like this song?

What do you think this song is about?

In the Bible, Jesus tells us that someday we're going to live with Him forever in a home big enough for God and all the people who love God.* What do you think of that?

Dear God,
Thank You that You're coming for us someday, to take me and _____ [your child's name] and all the people who love You to Your home.
Amen.

* John 14:2-3

## LET'S WRITE A POEM
# At the Zoo

Let's write a poem together, what do you say? And let's make it a silly one. Let's imagine a zoo, and that all the animals in the zoo got sick or came down with something. That would be a really bad day at the zoo, wouldn't it?

Let's see if we can fill in each blank with a word that rhymes with the animal who is getting sick. The first one is done for us.

*[Read the first two lines of the poem.]*

Do you hear that "measles" rhymes with "weasels"? Now let's do the rest.

It was a bad day at the zoo.

The weasels got the (<u>measles</u>).

The gnu got the _____.

The crickets got _____.

The fox got the _____.

The mice got _____.

The beavers got _____.

The snakes got the _____.

And I think I'm coming down with something, too! Achoo!

*[When you're finished filling in the blanks, read the entire poem, with you reading the first portion and your child saying the rhyming word at the end. If you need help, suggested rhymes are in the back of the book.]*

Do you know anyone who is sick today that we should pray for?

Let's thank God for being healthy, too.

Dear God,
Thank You that _____ *[your child's name]* and I are healthy today. Please take care of _____ *[name the sick people your child mentioned]* and help them to get better.
        Amen.

## LET'S LOOK AT NATURE
# Nutty Friends

*[You will need a nut in its shell—the kind you can easily open, like a peanut or a pistachio. If your child is allergic to nuts, is too young to eat a nut without choking, or has tried nuts and doesn't like them, place an appropriate treat in a small box and adapt what you say accordingly.]*

*[Show your child the nut in its shell.]*

If you didn't know what this was, would you think it was something good to eat? Explain.

*[Tap the shell, then let your child tap it.]*

This shell is hard, isn't it? That doesn't seem very good to eat.

*[Sniff the nut, then let your child sniff it.]*

It doesn't smell like cookies or spaghetti or anything else good to eat.

*[Open the nut.]*

Now what do you think: Would this be good to eat?

*[Let your child eat the nut.]*

Do you like it? Lots of people like nuts a lot. But you'd never know unless you took the trouble to find the good stuff inside the shell.

Sometimes people can be a little like nuts. Can you think of any of your friends that you weren't sure you'd like at first?

What made you think they might not be good friends?

What did you find out about them that made you like them?

Getting to know friends is kind of like opening up a nut, isn't it? You might not be sure you'll like them when you first look at them  That's like looking at the nut's shell. But when you take the trouble to find out the good stuff about them, you like them. That's like opening the nutshell to find out what's inside.

Can you think of anybody that you're not really friends with right now?

Do you think that you might get to be friends if you took the trouble to find out the good things about them?

Let's pray about that.

Dear God,
Thank You for _____'s *[your child's name]* friends:
for _____ *[name the friends your child mentioned]*.
Thank You that _____ *[your child's name]* got
to know them and got to be friends with them. We pray
for _____ *[name the children your child identified as not being friends]*. When _____ *[your child's name]* looks at them, those kids seem as if they
might not be very good friends. Please help _____
*[your child's name]* to take the trouble to get to know the
good things about _____ *[name the non-friends again]*.
Amen.

Just a Reminder . . .

### Special Future

Water has a hard time rising above its own level. Children can, too. But when children hear words from a parent, grandparent, or other loved one that picture a special future for them, they rise to those words. Helping your children see that God has a special future for them ( Jeremiah 29:11) and that you appreciate their unique character traits and talents can fill up their hearts with your blessing.

### LET'S PLAY A GAME
# Concentration

*[You will need a deck of cards—any type that includes matching pairs, such as "Old Maid," "Go Fish" "Uno," or "Pit."]*

This game is called Concentration.

*[Shuffle the cards and put them face down on the bed, arranged in a square or a rectangle. Then explain the rules as follows.]*

The game begins when the first player turns over any two cards to see if they match. If you turn over two "fours," you have found a match. If you turn over two with matching pictures, that's a match. When you find a match, you get to keep those two cards, and you get to turn over two more cards. If you don't find a match, it's my turn.

*[Play until all the cards are matched. The player with the most cards wins.]*

Why do you think this game is called "Concentration"? Do you know what that name means?

Sometimes this game is also called "Memory." Why do you think that's a good name for this game?

What's one thing you'd like me always to remember about you?

Here's one thing I want you always to remember about me: I love you!

And here's something you can remember about God: He loves you, too.

Let's talk to Him.

Dear God,
Thank You that we can concentrate and remember things. Help me to remember _____ *[name the thing your child mentioned]*. Help _____ *[your child's name]* always to remember that I love him/her. And help us both to remember that You love us. We love You, too.
      Amen.

### LET'S BE THANKFUL
# Ouchies

Do you have any "ouchies" today?

*[Use whatever word your child uses for scrapes or bruises. If your child doesn't have any wounds, ask him or her to think of a time he or she got hurt.]*

How did you get that one?

Have you ever thought of being thankful when something hurts?

When something hurts, sometimes it's God's way of telling us to be careful. For example, when you've touched a hot pan, what did you do with your hand?

*[Pantomime pulling your hand away from something hot.]*

Why do you pull your hand away from something hot?

What would have happened if you couldn't feel that being burned would hurt you?

Getting hurt is like God's hand pulling us away from something that would be bad for us. Sometimes our bodies get hurt. That warns us about something that could be bad for our bodies—like a hot pan.

Sometimes we feel hurt inside. Do you know how bad you feel inside when you tell a lie, or when you disobey? That hurt inside warns you that telling lies and disobeying are bad for you, too.

Have you ever felt bad inside like that?

*[Discuss your child's answer, then lead into a prayer like the one below.]*

Dear God,
Thank You that You warn us about things that are bad for our bodies, even if that warning hurts a little. Help _____ 's *[your child's name]* _____ *[name the scrape or bruise your child currently has]* to get better. And thank You that You warn us about things that are bad for us inside, too. Keep _____ *[your child's name]* safe and healthy on the inside, especially when he/she is tempted to _____ *[name the action your child described when you were talking about lying, etc.]*.
    Amen.

LET'S PLAY A GAME
# Hot and Cold

Tonight's game is Hot and Cold.

*[One person goes out of the room while the other person hides something—maybe a small toy. When it's hidden, the other person is called back into the room and starts looking. The one who hid the object gives hints when the other person asks for them.*

*If the person looking for the object is far away from it, the hint is the word "cold." If the person is really far away, the hint is either "really cold" or "freezing." The closer the person gets to the hidden object, the warmer the hints become. "Warm" would be in the general area. "Really warm" would be closer. "Hot" would be really close. "Melting hot" means the object is right under the person's nose.*

*The person who finds the object now gets to hide it. To make the game more fun, set a time limit—one or two minutes—using a watch or an egg timer.*

*When the game is over, lead into prayer with comments like the following.]*

Wouldn't it be nice if, every time you lost something, someone could give you clues to help you find it?

Did you know that God never loses track of you? If you were the hidden toy, and God were looking for you, God would always be "melting hot." He is always right where you are.

How does that make you feel?

Dear God,
Thank You that You never, ever lose _____
*[your child's name]*. Help him/her to feel safe and loved because You are always
with him/her.
    Amen.

### LET'S DO A PUZZLE
# Mystery Doodles

Look at the mystery doodles. Can you figure out what each one is? If you get stuck, look in the back of the book for the answers.

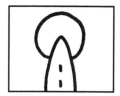 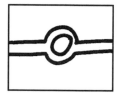 

Some people are like mystery doodles. When we look at them we just can't figure them out. Maybe we don't even like them.

For example, maybe you know a grown-up who is really strict. Like a teacher at school or Sunday school who is always telling you to be quiet. You look at that person and you think, "This is a crabby person."

But maybe the person isn't really crabby. Maybe the person just wants you to listen so you can learn something important. When you know that, you think, "This is a person who wants me to learn."

Can you think of anybody that you have trouble liking?

*[Let your child give an example, then talk about what reasons the person might have for the behavior that your child dislikes.]*

Let's pray for your "mystery doodle" person, and let's pray that we'll be able to see that person in a new way.

Dear God,

_____ *[your child's name]* sometimes has a hard time with _____ *[name the person your child identified as hard to like]*. Please help _____ *[your child's name]* to see that person as a "mystery doodle" person. Help _____ *[your child's name]* not to see him/her as _____ *[describe the actions your child dislikes]* but to see _____ *[describe the reasons you discussed for the person's behavior]*. Thank You that when You look at _____ *[your child's name]*, You notice all the good things about him/her.

Amen.

### LET'S DO AN EXPERIMENT
# Crystal Garden

*[You will need several charcoal briquettes (not the self-starting kind), a disposable pie pan, 1/4 cup of salt, 1/4 cup of laundry bluing, 1 tablespoon of ammonia, and a container for mixing the salt, bluing, and ammonia.]*

*[Show your child a charcoal briquette.]*

This isn't very pretty, is it?

*[Let your child smell the ammonia from a safe distance.]*

That's not a pretty smell, either, is it? Watch what I do now.

*[Arrange the briquettes in the disposable pie pan. Mix the ingredients and pour them over the briquettes, but don't entirely cover them with the mixture. By the morning, you should see crystals of many different shapes, sizes, and colors.]*

It still doesn't look very special, does it? But by tomorrow we will have something pretty out of these not-so-pretty things.

Sometimes God makes something wonderful come out of things that aren't very wonderful at all.

*[Share an experience you've had of God bringing good out of difficult circumstances.]*

Sometimes it takes a while to see how God makes good things out of bad things—just like it will take a while for us to see how our experiment makes something pretty out of these not-so-pretty things. But God always does bring good out of bad; He promised. Listen: "We know that in all things God works for the good of those who love him" (Romans 8:28a).

Thank You, God,
That in all things, even the bad things, You work for the good of those who love You. Thank You that You did that when _____ *[describe the situation you shared earlier].* Thank You that You will do that for _____ *[your child's name],* too.
    Amen.

*[When you leave the room, take the pie pan of charcoal with you so the odor does not disturb your child.]*

LET'S PLAY A GAME
# Build a Beetle

*[You will need one die, a pencil, and two pieces of paper.]*

The object of the game is to be the first to build a beetle. We take turns throwing the die. You get one roll, then you can draw whatever part of the beetle goes with the number on the die. You don't have to draw them in any particular order except that you can't draw the eyes or the feelers until you've rolled a 1 or 2 to draw the head. That's what makes it tricky!

Here are the things you get to draw with each number on the die:

For any number you roll, you get to draw the body.

Roll a 1 or 2, and you get to draw the head.

Roll a 3 or 6, and you get to draw 3 legs on one side of the body.

Roll another 3 or 6, and you get to draw the other 3 legs.

 Roll a 4, and you get to draw 1 feeler.

Roll another 4, and you get to draw the other feeler.

 Roll a 5, and you get to draw 1 eye.

Roll another 5, and you get to draw the other eye and win the game.

There! You've made a beetle! Of course, it doesn't move or eat or crawl around the way live beetles do. Only God can make those! Let's praise Him for all He's made.

Dear God,
Thank You for beetles and bunnies and bats and bananas. And thank You for _____
*[your child's name]*.
       Amen.

## LET'S TALK ABOUT FEELINGS
# Growing Pains

A lot of children get "growing pains." Do you know what "growing pains" are? They are the pains you get from your muscles being stretched. Growing pains feel like your body is growing faster than the muscles can, so the muscles feel stretched tight and sore.

*[Start rubbing your child's legs or arms.]*

Do you ever get growing pains?

Sometimes growing up seems hard. Maybe you get growing pains. Or maybe what seems hard is that you have more chores to do, like _____ *[name some of the chores your child has at home]*. Or maybe what's hard about growing up is that you are expected to be quiet and listen in church when you want to talk and play.

Does anything seem hard to you about growing up?

*[Listen to your child's responses.]*

Let's talk to God about it.

Dear Jesus,
Thank You that _____ *[your child's name]* is growing up, just as You made children to do. Thank You that his/her body is growing and that he/she is growing more responsible about chores. But some parts of growing up can seem hard. Please help _____ *[your child's name]* to handle _____ *[name the challenges your child mentioned]*. Thank You, Jesus, that You were a little child once and so You know all about growing up.

    Amen.

## LET'S PLANT A SEED
# God So Loved the World

*[You will need a slip of paper, a pencil, and a balloon.]*

*[If you planted bean seeds (page 34), look at the plants that are growing.]*

Let's plant another seed. Not a seed in a pot, but a seed in your heart. Do you remember that Jesus said God's Word is like a seed planted in your heart?

Here is a Bible verse to learn by heart:

"For God so loved the world that He gave His one and only Son, that whoever believes in Him shall not perish but have eternal life" (John 3:16, NIV).

*[Read the verse and have your child repeat it.]*

Who is the Son that God gave?

What do you think it means to believe in Jesus?

Do you know what "perish" means?

This verse promises that anyone who loves and believes in Jesus doesn't have to worry about what happens after they die because they will live forever with Jesus!

*[If you consider it appropriate at this time, ask your child if he or she believes in Jesus and would like to pray to ask Jesus to live in his or her heart.]*

Let's see if you can tell me the verse so I can write it on this paper.

*[Have your child recite the verse again as you print it. Roll up the paper and put it inside the balloon. Blow up the balloon or have your child blow it up, then tie the end.]*

Tomorrow, if you can say the verse correctly, you can pop the balloon and free the verse.

Dear God,
Thank You that You love _____ *[your child's name]* so much You were willing to give Your one and only Son to give _____ *[your child's name]* eternal life. Help _____ *[your child's name]* always to love and believe in Jesus. In Jesus' name we pray.
　　　　Amen.

### LET'S PLAY A GAME
# Simon Says

Tonight's game is Simon Says.

*[The two of you alternate who plays Simon. When Simon tells the other person what to do, the person must do it. For example, the person who is Simon starts out by saying, "Simon says, 'Put your hand on your head.'" The person who is Simon must act out the command first. The other person must respond by putting his hand on his head. But if Simon says, "Put your hand on your head," without first using the words, "Simon says," the other player should not follow the command. If a player can go 10 times without a mistake, that player wins the right to be Simon.]*

What would it be like if in real life you weren't supposed to obey instructions unless I or your teacher or someone else said, "Simon says," first? Would it be confusing?

Do you think you'd make some mistakes?

"Simon" in the game Simon Says tries to confuse us. But God doesn't try to confuse us. He wants us to obey Him all the time. And God wants you to obey your parents and teachers and other grown-ups in charge. You might not always like doing what they say, but at least you know you are supposed to obey!

Dear God,
We like playing games together. But we're glad that You don't play games to confuse us about when to obey You. Help _____ *[your child's name]* always to obey You. Help me always to obey You, too. And help me give _____ *[your child's name]* good directions for him/her to obey—all the time.

  Amen.

### LET'S TALK ABOUT THE DAY
# Thinking about God

*[Before you begin this blessing, decide on a form of meaningful touch that you can give to your child and then your child can give to you. Some ideas include:*

• *Lightly brush your fingertips up and down your child's arm;*

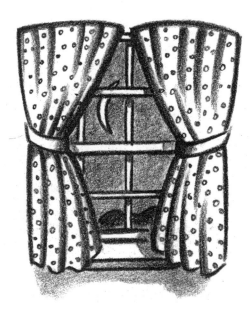

• *Rub your child's back or shoulders;*

• *Smooth your child's hair.]*

Let's talk about each other's day. While you talk, I'll lightly brush my fingertips up and down your arm *[or whatever form of touch you've chosen].* When you're finished, I'll tell you about my day, and you can brush your fingertips up and down my arm.

So tell me: How was your day?

Did you have any thoughts today about God? If so, would you like to share them?

What are some of the things you prayed about today?

*[Now change roles and let your child ask you about your day.]*

Dear God,
Thank You for this day and for all the thoughts we had of You during it. Thank You that You listen to _____'s *[your child's name]* prayers for \_\_\_\_ _____ *[list the things your child prayed about today].* In Jesus' name we pray.

Amen.

LET'S PLANT A SEED
# Becoming Like Jesus

*[You will need a pencil.]*

*[If you planted bean seeds (page 34), look at the plants that are growing.]*

Let's plant another seed. Not a seed in a pot, but a seed in your heart. Do you remember that Jesus said God's Word is like a seed planted in your heart?

Here is a Bible verse to learn by heart:

"God planned that those He had chosen would become like His Son" (Romans 8:29a).

*[Read the verse and have your child repeat it.]*

Let's rewrite that verse to make sure you know what it means about you. First, let's put your name in the first blank.

*[If your child can write his or her name, let him or her write it in the blank in the verse below. Otherwise, you can write it for your child.]*

"God planned that _____ would become like _____:

- •
- •
- •

    •

    •

    •

Now we need to fill in the other blank with another name. The name of God's Son goes in that blank. Do you know His name?

*[After your child responds, write "Jesus" in the second blank in the verse on the previous page.]*

What do you know about Jesus? What is He like?

*[As your child responds, fill in the spaces behind the bullets above with the qualities that can also apply to Jesus' followers: for example, kind, loving, good. If your child names attributes that only God has, like "He can do anything; He is God," affirm those answers but don't write them down. Write down qualities Jesus will ultimately give to Christians, like "perfect" and "live forever" and explain to your child that this is part of his or her promised future.]*

Let's read the verse the way we've rewritten it.

*[Read the personalized verse with the descriptions of what it means to be like Jesus.]*

How does it feel to know that God has planned this special future for you?

Let's thank Him for your future.

Dear God,
Thank You for the special future You have decided on ahead of time for _____ *[your child's name].*
Thank You that You have chosen _____
*[your child's name]* to be like Jesus—to be _____
*[repeat the qualities you listed above].* How exciting!
  Amen.

### LET'S LOOK AT NATURE
# Hair

Let's talk about hair.

*[Peer at your child's hair, then put your head—or arm if you have no hair on your head—near your child's face for him or her to examine.]*

Why do you think God gave us hair?

*[Some reasons could be to keep our head warm, to keep particles out of our eyes, to filter dust from our nose.]*

How many hairs do you think I have on my head? Try counting them.

Give up? Jesus said that God knows the exact number of hairs on your head.* That's how well He knows you! Pretty incredible, isn't it?

Dear God,
Thank You that You love _____ *[your child's name]* so much that You even keep track of how many hairs he/she has on his/her head.

      Amen.

---

* Matthew 10:30; Luke 12:7.

### LET'S PLAY A GAME
## Boxes

*[You will need a pencil.]*

*[In this game you connect the dots on the grid on the opposite page. The two of you alternate drawing a line to connect two dots. The one who gets to complete the final side of a box gets to put his or her initial in the box. The player with the most boxes when all the dots are connected is the winner. After the game, lead into prayer with questions like the following.]*

How does it feel to finish off a box and put your initial in it?

I feel pretty good about finishing these boxes, and I feel pretty good about finishing projects I start during the day, too. Like today, I felt good about _____ *[list some things you accomplished in the day, such as making supper, getting things wrapped up at work so you could come home to the family, etc.].*

What did you feel good about doing today?

*[Help your child think of some successes, which could include having fun playing a game, building an interesting structure with Legos® or blocks, or getting a chore done.]*

Let's thank God for the things we did today.

Dear God,
Thanks for the things we feel good about today. Thank You that _____ *[your child's name]* could _____ *[list the successes your child men-tioned]*. Thank You for the things we can do tomorrow.
     Amen.

## LET'S WRITE A LETTER TO GOD
# Doing the Best I Can

*[You will need a pencil.]*

Here's one of my favorite letters to God, written by a little boy named Frank.

> Dear God,
>     I'm doing the best I can.
>                 Frank*

Why don't you write a letter, too? You can use the space across the page. Write to God and tell Him about some area of your life that you're really working at.

*[If your child cannot write, have him or her dictate the letter to you.]*

Now, why don't you pray that letter to God in your own words? You don't have to read your letter, just tell God what you want Him to know.

*[Let your child pray, then conclude with a prayer like the following.]*

*From Children's Letters to God: The New Collection compiled by Stuart Hample and Eric Marshall (Workman Publishing, 1991).

124

Dear God,
Thank You that _____ *[your child's name]* is so special to You that You always listen to him/her. You know
that _____ *[your child's name]* is doing the best
he/she can at _____ *[list the things your child
mentioned in the letter]*. Thank You that he/she is getting
better and better at it.
     Amen.


Dear God,

_____

_____

_____

_____

_____

_____

_____

_____

_____

_____

### LET'S HEAR A STORY
# Poodle Pride

This is a story about the poodle's hairdo.

A poodle walked out of a poodle beauty parlor with his hair washed, trimmed, and perfectly brushed. He straightened his collar, held his nose up high, and pranced down the sidewalk.

"A bone for a poor dog," begged a mutt.

"Disgusting," thought the poodle. "He ought to be put in some kennel." As he passed, he raised his nose even higher.

Then he caught sight of a dog sunning himself on the sidewalk. "He should be put to sleep," thought the poodle as he sniffed the air proudly.

He turned the corner where a pack of dogs was standing around a fire hydrant. He pranced right past them, thinking, "The dogs of the street are so, so ordinary—not fine poodles like me."

He raised his nose still higher. But with his nose so high in the air, he didn't see that a manhole cover had been removed by workmen. And he fell into the sewer. What can we learn from this poodle?

Listen to this Bible verse: "If you are proud, you will fall" (Proverbs 16:18b). How does that remind you of the poodle?

Why did the poodle think he was so good?

Would you want a friend who acted like that proud poodle?

What are some things you are good at?

Do you think people would want you for a friend if you act like you're better than anybody else because you are good at those things?

How could you use the things you're good at to help other people?

Let's pray about not acting like we're better than anybody else.

Dear God,
Thank You that _____ [your child's name] is good at _____ [name the strengths your child identified]. Help him/her to use those abilities to help other people, not to be like that proud poodle who thought he was better than anybody else.
     Amen.

LET'S LOOK AT NATURE
# Talking Without Words

*[Often when your child asks questions, especially questions
about God, the child is not looking for a scientific answer
but a more personal answer. For example, when a child
asks why the grass is green, you could say because it has
within it a substance called chlorophyll, which gives it that
color. And you would be right. But you could also use that
question as a starting point to talk about what you learn
about God from the grass He made. For instance, you learn
that God takes care of sheep and horses and rabbits by giving them grass to eat. You could talk about how it feels to
play barefoot in the grass and reflect together on whether
God takes delight in His creatures' pleasure. Take some
time tonight to reflect on nature from the perspective of
what it reveals about God.]*

Maybe you know that one of the best ways to learn
about God is by what He tells us in the Bible. But did
you know that we can learn about God by looking at
nature, too? How do I know? The Bible says so! Listen:

"The heavens tell about the glory of God. The skies
show that His hands created them. Day after day they
speak about it. Night after night they make it known.
But they don't speak or use words. No sound is heard
from them" (Psalm 19:1-3).

Let's think about how nature could tell us about God—without even using any words.

I know something God made in the sky: the sun. What does the sun do? What does that tell you about God?

*[For example, the sun gives us light—a powerful thing to a child afraid of the dark. The sun makes us warm, which shows God cares about our comfort.]*

What else can you think of that God made? What can you learn about God from that?

*[Continue your conversation until you're ready to pray. If the only conclusion your child draws is that God sure did make a lot of stuff that nobody else could make—well, that's not a bad theology lesson for one night.]*

Dear God,
You are so wonderful that even the skies want to tell about You! Thank You that You made _____
*[name some things you talked about]* to _____
*[name some things from your discussion about what nature reveals about God].* Thank You, God, for the wonderful world where You have put us. Help our lives to be just as wonderful and just as beautiful and to tell others about You.

     Amen.

## LET'S DO AN EXPERIMENT
# Soap Chase

*[You will need a cup of water, pepper, and liquid soap.]*

*[While your child watches, sprinkle pepper on the surface of the water.]*

What do you think will happen if I drop a little soap in the water?

*[After your child has made a prediction, add a few drops of soap to the cup. The pepper will zoom away across the surface of the water.]*

The Bible tells us that sin is like dirty spots in our hearts—kind of like the way the pepper looked like spots on the water.

But when we tell Jesus about our sins—about the things we've done wrong—and ask Him to forgive us, He washes our hearts clean and chases the sin away—even better than the soap chased the pepper away.

Do you have anything you want to ask Jesus to forgive you for?

*[Gently guide your child to recognize his or her sin—perhaps unkind treatment of a friend or family member, perhaps disobedience to you. Use this time not to berate your child but to let him or her experience confession and forgiveness.]*

Let's ask Jesus to forgive you for those things. Would you like to say the prayer, or would you like me to say it for you?

*[Let your child pray or pray on his or her behalf, then close with a prayer like the following.]*

Dear Jesus,
Thank You that You love _____ *[your child's name]* even when he/she sins. Thank You that now You have washed _____'s *[your child's name]* heart cleaner than soap and chased the sin right out.
    Amen.

### LET'S PLAY A GAME
# Squiggles

*[You will need some crayons and several pieces of paper.]*

*[To play this game, one of you draws a squiggle of some kind on a piece of paper. The other makes a picture out of it.*

*For example, one of you draws a squiggle, like this:*

*And the other one turns the squiggle into a picture, like this:*

*Go back and forth as many times as you like. Then lead
into prayer with questions like the following.]*

Which is your favorite squiggle drawing?

Which squiggle do you think looked the weirdest before
we turned it into a picture?

You know, sometimes I feel a little squiggly. Sometimes I
feel like a weird wiggle that isn't really much of a picture. But God is a terrific artist. Because He is in charge
of my life, I know He's turning my squiggles into master-
pieces. And I know He's doing that for you, too.

Dear God,
It's fun to see squiggles turn into pictures. And it's fun to
see You working in _____'s *[your child's name]*
to make him/her into the wonderful, loving person You
want him/her to be. Thank You for the plans You have
for making _____ *[your child's name]* into a
masterpiece.
        Amen.

### LET'S MAKE SOMETHING
# W.W.J.D. Bracelet

*[You will need two fat rubber bands and a pen.]*

Tonight, let's write something on a rubber band and put it around our wrists to remind us of something really important. Let's print the letters W. W. J. D. The letters stand for the words, "What Would Jesus Do?"

*[Help your child print the letters on a rubber band, or print them for your child. Make a bracelet for yourself, too.]*

When we look at our bracelets, these letters are supposed to remind us to treat other people the way Jesus would treat them. Do you have any ideas of what that would be like?

Jesus gave us a good way to figure out W.W.J.D.— to figure out what Jesus would do and what we should do. Listen to what He said in a sermon He preached on a hillside:

"In everything, do to others what you would want them to do to you" (Matthew 7:12).

Let's think about how we could do that tomorrow.

*[Talk with your child about a situation in which you know he or she has difficulty responding appropriately—perhaps an ongoing clash with a sibling or a friend that you have observed.]*

Let's ask Jesus to help us remember tomorrow to do what He would do.

Dear Jesus,
Help us to do to others what we would want them to do to us. When _____ *[your child's name]* looks at his/her W.W.J.D. bracelet tomorrow, help him/her remember to _____
*[name some of the actions you and your child discussed].*
Thank You that _____ *[your child's name]* can grow to be more and more like You!
        Amen.

*[You can follow up on this activity tomorrow with "W.W.J.D. Today?" (p. 136).]*

LET'S TALK ABOUT THE DAY
# W.W.J.D. Today?

*[Use this activity the day after you've done "W.W.J.D. Bracelet" (p. 134).]*

*[Before you begin this blessing, decide on a form of meaningful touch that you can give to your child and then your child can give to you. Some ideas include:*

- *Lightly brush your fingertips up and down your child's arm;*

- *Rub your child's back or shoulders;*

- *Smooth your child's hair.]*

Let's talk about each other's day. While you talk, I'll lightly brush my fingertips up and down your arm *[or whatever form of touch you've chosen]*. When you're finished, I'll tell you about my day, and you can brush your fingertips up and down my arm.

Tell me how the "What Would Jesus Do?" reminder made a difference in your day.

*[Discuss your child's day, asking specifically about the situation you talked about last night. Then trade roles and talk about how your W.W.J.D. bracelet served as a reminder for you.]*

Let's pray about those things.

Dear Jesus,
Thank You for the wonderful future You have planned
for _____ *[your child's name]*. Thank You that
You are making him/her more and more like You. And
thank You that today _____ *[your child's
name]* had a chance to practice being like You when
_____ *[name the situation you discussed]*.
    Amen.

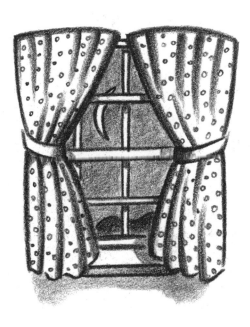

LET'S LOOK IN THE BIBLE
# The Most Important Commandment

*[You will need a Bible.]*

If you had to pick the most important commandment or instruction in the Bible, what would you say it is?

*[Listen to your child's suggestions, affirming their importance.]*

All the instructions in the Bible are important. But somebody asked Jesus that question once. Let's read about it.

*[Read Mark 12:28-31.]*

What part of Jesus' answer do you think is the most important commandment?

*[Help your child identify loving God as most important.]*

How do you show God that you love Him?

Dear God,
Thank You that _____ *[your child's name]* shows his/her love for You by _____ *[name the ways your child identified as showing love]*. Thank You that You love _____ *[your child's name]* very, very much! And help _____ *[your child's name]* to know how much I love him/her, too.
        Amen.

### LET'S PLANT A SEED
# Love the Lord

*[Use this blessing after you've done "The Most Important Commandment" (p. 138).]*

Let's plant another seed—in your heart. Here is a Bible verse to learn:

"Love the Lord your God with all your soul and with all your mind and with all your strength" (Mark 12:30, NIV).

*[Read verse and have your child repeat it.]*

Jesus said this was the greatest commandment of all! So it's a good one to learn by heart.

Count how many times you see the word "all" in this verse.

God wants us to love Him with ALL of ourselves!

What's one thing could you do tomorrow to show God you love Him?

Dear Lord,
Help us to love You with all of our whole selves. And help _____ *[your child's name]* to show You tomorrow that he/she loves You by _____ *[name the action your child proposed]*. Thank You that You love _____ *[your child's name]*—ALL of him/her!
    Amen.

## LET'S PLAY A GAME
# Lost in Bed

Let's play the game, "Find the Lost Child." Here's how we play. I'll go out of the room, and you hide under your covers. I'll go out in the hall and give you 15 seconds to get covered up really well in bed, and then I'll come looking for you. You have to be really quiet and really still. Because if I find you, I'm going to tickle you!

*[Leave the room and count down from 15: 15, 14, 13.... When you come back in the room, make a big deal of looking for your child in various places, both likely (in the closet) and unlikely (in the sock drawer). Carry on a running narration of your search, making sure to mention how lost your child is. The more you draw it out, the more fun it will be for your child. Finally, find your child and do your tickling! Then make a transition to prayer with questions like the following.]*

How could you get lost in your own bed?

Did you think I would ever find you?

It was pretty silly, wasn't it, that I was looking all over when I'd told you to hide in your bed. So I really knew where you were, didn't I?

God always knows where you are. Not just when you're in bed, but all the time! Even when you get really lost, God can find you! And He always will.

Let's pray to Him.

Dear God,
Thank You that You always know where _____
*[your child's name]* is. Thank You that You will never, ever lose him/her!
      Amen.

## LET'S PRETEND
# Scary Shadows

*[You'll need flashlight, construction paper, and scissors.]*

Let's close our eyes. Imagine we're walking in the woods.

*[Take your child's hand, but stay on the bed.]*

I'm pretending that I see a deer in the woods. What do you see?

*[Let your child share some imaginary sights.]*

I think I hear a woodpecker going rat-a-tat-tat on a tree. What sounds do you hear? Now open your eyes. Why don't you draw some of the animals we might see on a walk in the woods, and I will cut them out.

*[When you've finished, turn off the lights and turn on the flashlight.]*

Let's go walking through the woods again, this time with our eyes open. Oh, look! What's that?

*[Shine the flashlight on the figure of one of the animals, projecting its shadow onto the wall. After you've done a few, let your child use the flashlight.]*

If we were *really* in the woods at night, do you think any of these shadows would be a little scary? Which ones?

*[After your child responds, gently squeeze his or her hand.]*

You know that if we were *really* in the woods at night, I'd hold your hand tight and keep you safe.

What are some of the things that sometimes seem scary to you?

*[Listen to your child's fears without trying to explain them away.]*

Did you know that God stays right with you to keep you safe when you are scared? Listen to what David wrote in the Bible about being scared: "Even though I walk through the darkest valley, I will not be afraid. You [God] are with me" (Psalm 23:4a).

How does it make you feel to know that God is taking care of you, even in the scary times?

*[Listen to your child's responses, then move into the blessing prayer below.]*

Dear God,
Thank You that I can hold _____'s *[your child's name]* hand and keep him/her safe. And thank You that You love _____ *[your child's name]* so much that You stay with him/her no matter how scary things get. Next time _____ *[your child's name]* gets scared about _____ *[list some of the fears your child mentioned]*, help him/her to remember that You are taking care of him/her.
    Amen.

LET'S TALK ABOUT THE DAY
# Something New

*[Before you begin this blessing, decide on a form of meaningful touch that you can give to your child and then your child can give to you. Some ideas include:*

*• Lightly brush your fingertips up and down your child's arm;*

*• Rub your child's back or shoulders;*

*• Smooth your child's hair.]*

Let's talk about each other's day. While you talk, I'll lightly brush my fingertips up and down your arm *[or whatever form of touch you've chosen]*. When you're finished, I'll tell you about my day, and you can brush your fingertips up and down my arm.

So tell me. How was your day?

Did you do anything new today?

Did you learn anything new today?

*[Talk about your child's response, focusing especially on new experiences, thoughts, or feelings.]*

The Bible tells us about something new we can look for every day. Listen: "[God's] great love is new every morning" (Lamentations 3:23a).

How did you see God's love today?

*[Now change roles and tell your child about something new you experienced or learned today, and especially about how you experienced God's love.]*

Let's thank God for His love.

Dear God,
Thank You for the new day You gave us today! Thank You that _____ *[your child's name]* could _____ *[describe an experience your child mentioned]*. Thank You that You love _____ *[your child's name]* and that You will send a whole new day full of Your love tomorrow!
    Amen.

*145*

### LET'S DO AN EXPERIMENT
# Little Lightning

*[You will need a balloon.]*

*[Try this experiment by yourself before doing it with your child. If the humidity level in your home is too high, the experiment won't work.]*

Have you ever wondered what lightning is? Tonight we're going to find out. Tonight we're going to make our *own* lightning. Our lightning will be so small, we probably won't be able to see it, but we'll be able to hear it if we listen very carefully.

*[Rub the balloon vigorously on your child's bedspread or blanket, then have your child bring his or her hand close to the balloon. You will hear a tiny popping sound.]*

Did you hear the sound? Not very scary, was it? Not like lightning and thunder. But actually it *is* like lightning, because what made the sound was static electricity.

Sometimes when you scuff your feet on a rug and reach for a doorknob, you get a shock. That's the same sort of thing. It's static electricity.

Lightning in the sky is like static electricity between the clouds. It's almost as if the clouds are giving each other shocks. And those shocks are the lightning.

Let's think of some things we could tell the clouds when we want the lightning to stop. How about, "Hey, clouds! Quit shocking each other up there!"

What else could we tell the clouds?

Do you think we can make the lightning stop?

Do you know who can make the lightning stop? God, of course, because God is in charge of the whole wide world.

Dear God Almighty,
You are stronger than the scariest of storms! You are strong enough to make lightning and strong enough to make it stop. And You are strong enough to take care of
_____ [your child's name] in even the scariest storm. Please give him/her a good night's sleep tonight.
     Amen.

### LET'S PRETEND
# Storm Tracking

*[You will need a flashlight.]*

Let's pretend a storm is coming our way.

This will be the lightning.

*[Flash the flashlight on and off.]*

And this will be the thunder.

*[Make your most impressive thundering sound.]*

My job will be to make the storm. Your job will be to figure out how far away the storm is. This is how you do it.

You see, lightning and thunder happen at the same time, but since light travels so much faster than sound, you see the lightning before you hear the thunder. Here's how you figure how far away it is. The moment you see the lightning, start counting like this:

"And one and, and two and, and three and". . . and keep counting until you hear the thunder. Whatever number you're at when you hear the thunder is about how many miles away the storm is.

*[Turn off the light, stand at the other side of the room, and shine the flashlight on and off. Prompt your child to start counting. About ten seconds later let out a loud sound of thunder. Now turn on the light.]*

How far away was the storm?

*[Repeat this process as many times as you like, letting your child create the "storm" if he or she wishes. Then make a transition to prayer with questions and comments like the following.]*

How far away do you like storms to be?

Do you ever feel scared when storms get close?

What helps you when you're feeling scared?

How far away do you think God is when there's a storm?

Dear God,
Thank You that, no matter how close or far away a storm is, You are always right here with _____
*[your child's name]*, keeping him/her safe.
     Amen.

## LET'S WRITE A LETTER TO GOD
# I Wonder...

*[You will need a pencil.]*

Here's a letter a young girl once wrote to God:

Dear God,
I know all about where babies come from—I think. From inside mommies, and daddies put them there. Where are they before that? Do You have them in heaven? How do they get down here? Do You have to take care of them all first? Please answer all my questions. I always think of You.
> Yours truly,
> Susan*

Those are pretty good questions, aren't they?

*[If you have been looking for an opening to talk with your child about where babies come from, you can do so now. Otherwise, you can simply move on to ask what questions your child would like to ask God.]*

What questions would you like to ask God?

Let's write a letter to God and put some of *your* questions in it, okay? We'll use the space across the page.

---

*From *Children's Letters to God: The New Collection* compiled by Stuart Hample and Eric Marshall (Workman Publishing, 1991).

*[If your child doesn't know how to write, have your child dictate a letter. When you're finished, let your child draw a picture on the page. If you can help answer questions from your child's letter, do so—or promise to research the matter. If the questions aren't answerable, explain that you can both look forward to asking God about them in heaven.]*

_____

_____

_____

_____

_____

Dear God,
Thank You that _____'s *[your child's name]*
questions are important to You and that You're never too
busy to listen to him/her.
     Amen.

LET'S HEAR A STORY
# A Mad, Mean Meal

Once upon a time, a family of raccoons lived in a hut by a stream. Every evening the family fished together for the dinner meal, which was always pleasant. The parents talked nicely to the children, and the children talked nicely to the parents, for they all loved each other.

One day, though, the river dried up, and there were no fish. The family gathered what vegetables they could, but these little raccoons were so hungry for a fat fish or a tasty hamburger!

"Can I spend the night with the bear cub down the road?" asked one of the young ones, because he knew the bears had meat every night.

"OK," said Mama Raccoon, "but first give me a big hug."

*[Give your child a hug.]*

The bears had a huge pile of hamburgers and ten extra-large, extra-cheese pizzas. The bears reached their big paws across the table, helping themselves, and their elbows kept bumping the little raccoon.

At last he asked politely, "Will someone please pass—"

"Get it yourself," snapped Father Bear.

As the little raccoon reached for a piece of pizza, one of the younger bears growled. The raccoon quickly pulled back his hand.

Suddenly, a fight broke out as two of the cubs were tugging at the same piece of pizza. Father Bear knocked them both off their stools. "Settle down, or I'll have a rug made out of you!"

The mad, mean talk lasted all through the meal. Finally, the raccoon asked to go home. When he got home, he threw his arms around his parents.

*[Have your child hug you.]*

They fixed him a bowl of leftover vegetables. His food never tasted so good as it did that night!

Where would you rather eat: at the bears' house or at the raccoons' house? Why?

Listen to this verse from the Bible: "A meal of vegetables where there is love is better than the finest meat where there is hatred" (Proverbs 15:17). Did the raccoons have a meal of vegetables with love, or fine meat with hatred?

Did the bears have a meal with love or with hatred?

Would you rather have a plain old sandwich at our house where we love you, or a terrific pizza *[or some other favorite food]* where people are yelling at you all the time?

Let's thank God that we have love at our supper table, even on the nights when you're not crazy about the food we're eating.

Dear God,
Thank You for the love we have in our home. Thank You that _____ *[list the members of your family]* love _____ *[your child's name]*. Help _____ *[your child's name]* to enjoy that love even when supper is _____ *[name your child's least favorite food]*!
　　　　Amen.

Just a Reminder . . .

### Genuine Commitment

In a world full of insecurity, knowing that a loving parent or grandparent will always be there for them gives children a tangible sense of stability. Helping children understand that their Heavenly Father will always be there for them builds their lives on the Rock.

### LET'S PLANT A SEED
# Give Thanks No Matter What

*[If you planted bean seeds (page 34), look at the plants that are growing.]*

Let's plant another seed. Not a seed in a pot, but a seed in your heart. Do you remember that Jesus said God's Word is like a seed planted in your heart?

Here is a Bible verse to learn by heart:

"Give thanks no matter what happens. God wants you to thank Him because you believe in Christ Jesus" (1 Thessalonians 5:17).

*[Read the verse and have your child repeat it.]*

What good thing happened today that you can say thanks to God for?

*[Offer a prayer of thanks, or guide your child to offer a prayer of thanks, for the things your child mentions.]*

Did anything happen today that wasn't so good?

*[If your child can't think of anything, suggest a frustrating situation you observed your child facing today, or mention someone you know who is sick or in some other way in a difficult situation.]*

Our verse says God wants us to give thanks no matter what happens. Even when things happen that we don't like. What could we find to say thanks to God about when _____
*[name one of the difficult situa-*
*tions you mentioned]?*

*[Help your child offer a prayer*
*of thanks. For example, if*
*your child hurt himself or*
*herself today, you could*
*give thanks for the person who*
*gave a hug and a bandage.*
*Conclude with a blessing prayer like the following.]*

Dear God,
Thank You for the good things that happened today.
Thank You that You were with _____
*[your child's name]* when the bad things happened,
too. Thank You that You will love and take care of
_____ *[your child's name]* no matter
what happens.
    Amen.

## LET'S DO AN EXPERIMENT
# "Seeing" the Wind

Let's do some experiments about wind. Since we can't make the wind come and go, we'll use our breath for wind.

Here's experiment number 1: Close your eyes, and tell me when the wind is blowing.

*[While your child's eyes are closed, blow on his or her cheek.]*

How did you know that the wind was blowing?

Here's experiment number 2: Watch this book and tell me when the wind is blowing.

*[Blow so that the pages of the book move.]*

How did you know that the wind was blowing?

Now let's think about what you learned. Can you see the wind?

*[If your child says he or she can, help him or her distinguish between seeing the wind and seeing what the wind does—in this case, ruffle the pages of the book.]*

If you can't see the wind, how do you know that it's real?

Now let's think about God. Can you see God?

If you can't see God, how do you know that He's real?

Remember how you could feel the wind when I blew on your cheek? Well, you can feel God's love when He takes care of you. What are some ways that God takes care of you?

Remember how you knew the wind was real because you could see it moving the pages? Well, you know God is real when you see what He does or what He makes. What are some things God has made?

Let's talk to God.

Dear God,
Even though we can't see You, we know You are here. We see the things You made, like _____ *[name some of the things your child mentioned]*. We feel You taking care of us when _____ *[mention some of your child's examples]*. Help _____ *[your child's name]* always to know You are real and that You love him/her.
　　　Amen.

### LET'S PLAY A GAME
# Sailboat

*[You will need two straws and a bottle cap or something similar that can float.]*

*[Play this game at the bathroom sink.]*

The object of the game is to blow the boat (this bottle cap) safely to the far shoreline without sinking it. You want to blow it to my side of the sink, and I want to blow it to your side of the sink.

*[Give your child a straw and you take the other one. Put the bottle cap in the middle of the sink. Then start blowing. Play as many times as you like, then go to the child's bed and make a transition to prayer with questions like the following.]*

Was it easier or harder than you thought it would be to make the boat go where you wanted?

Do you know how real boats are steered? The captain of a boat steers it with a rudder—just a small part of the boat that can turn in the water.

The Bible talks about rudders. Listen: "How about ships? They are very big. They are driven along by strong winds. But they are steered by a very small rudder. It makes them go where the captain wants to go. In the same way, the tongue is a small part of the body" (James 3:4-5a).

What are some good things you can say with your tongue?

What are some bad things you might say with your tongue?

If your tongue is like a rudder that steers a ship, then the good things you say steer you in a good way. But the bad things you say steer you in a bad way.

Let's ask God to help us say good things.

Dear God,
Thank You for giving _____ *[your child's name]* a tongue to talk with. Thank You for all the good things he/she says with that tongue, like _____ *[list some of the good things your child mentioned]*. Thank You especially that we can use our tongues to say, "I love you." We love You, God.
      Amen.

### LET'S TALK ABOUT THE DAY
# What If...

*[Before you begin this blessing, decide on a form of meaningful touch that you can give to your child. Some ideas include:*

- *Lightly brush your fingertips up and down your child's arm;*

- *Rub your child's back or shoulders;*

- *Smooth your child's hair.]*

Let's talk about the day. Only tonight, instead of talking about the day that really happened, let's talk about the day that might have happened.

*[Choose as many or as few of the following conversation-starters as you like, or make up your own.]*

What if you'd awakened this morning and found that your toys had come alive?

What if you'd been the parent today and you were in charge at our house?

What if you'd been able to have three wishes come true?

*[When you're ready to pray, make a transition with a question and comments like the following.]*

What would be the most wonderful part of what you've been imagining?

Did you know that the future God has planned for you will be even more wonderful than anything you can imagine?* That's a promise!

Dear God,
Thank You that You have a wonderful future planned for
_____ *[your child's name]*—even more wonderful than _____ *[name the wonderful things your child imagined]*.
     Amen.

* 1 Corinthians 2:9

### LET'S WRITE A SONG
## Food Fun

*[You will need a pencil.]*

Let's write a song thanking God for the food you like to eat. You name some of the things you like to eat, and I'll write them down.

*[Write your child's suggestions in the blanks on the opposite page. If you can match the number of syllables to the number of blanks, your song will have the same meter as "Mary Had a Little Lamb." If your child is in one of those stages in which he or she will eat only one food—say, peanut butter on white bread with the crusts cut off—fill in all the blanks with that one food. In a song, repetition can be good! When you've filled in the blanks, sing the song to the tune of "Mary Had a Little Lamb." If your child is full of ideas, you can use the same format to write several stanzas, either about food or about more things to be thankful for. When you're done singing together, pray the following blessing prayer.]*

"Thank You, God, for Food to Eat"
*[Sung to the tune of "Mary Had a Little Lamb"]*

Thank You, God, for food to eat,

_____ _____ _____

_____ _____ _____.

Thank You, God, for food to eat,

for _____ _____ _____ _____ _____.

Dear God,
Thank You that You take such good care of
_____ *[your child's name]*. Thank You
that You give him/her good food to eat every day.
Thank You that we have enough to eat. Thank You
especially for _____ *[name the foods
your child listed]*. Please take care of those children
who don't have enough to eat.
Amen.

### LET'S TALK ABOUT FEELINGS
# Fun with Faces

Faces are wonderful things. They can give us clues about what someone is feeling like inside. Look at this face.

*[Make a sad face.]*

If you saw my face like that, how do you think I would be feeling?

If you're angry, what will your face look like?

*[Let your child show you.]*

If you're scared, how might it show on your face?

Happy?

Surprised?

What kind of a face would you use to show someone that you want to be friends?

What do you like best about your face?

Tonight I'm going to draw your face. It's really very easy. But it kind of tickles a little sometimes! Close your eyes, and I'll "draw" your face.

*[Lightly trace the oval of your child's face, then one by one trace the individual features—eyes, eyebrows, ears, nose, and lips.]*

Dear God,
Thank You for the faces You've given us. I love
_____ *[your child's name]* so much that
I just love to look at his/her face. Thank You for how
good _____ *[your child's name]* can make
people feel when he/she shows them his/her friendly
face.
    Amen.

LET'S PLAY A GAME
# Chewable Checkers

*[You will need a checker board and two kinds of food to use as checkers.]*

*[Gather your edible checkers with your child right before bedtime so your child can have a choice of snacks. You could use round crackers vs. square ones, white grapes vs. red grapes, O-shaped cereal vs. square cereal, carrot slices vs. celery slices, or whatever you decide.]*

*[Make up your own rules about how the snacks should be eaten. You probably won't want to eat all of them. You might want to eat the first piece captured and the fifth one, and the winner gets the last piece, or some other variation.]*

Who won this game?

Was the game fun for the winner?

Do you think the game was fun for the person who didn't win?

What made this game fun for both of us?

*[Talk a little with your child about having fun in the playing, not just in the winning, of a game. Of course, eating the game pieces makes that easier!]*

When we play games, it's important to be "good sports." Good sports are kind when they win; they don't make fun of the other player who didn't win. And good sports are pleasant when they don't win; they don't pout or whine or get mad because they didn't win.

Here's something good sports can say when they win and when they don't win. They can say, "Good game. I had fun playing with you."

*[Say that to your child and have your child say it back to you. Add a high five or a handshake.]*

Dear God,
Thank You that _____ *[your child's name]* was a good sport tonight. Thank You for the fun we have together, no matter who wins.
     Amen.

LET'S PRAY FOR OTHERS
# Praying for People We Love

*[You will need a pencil.]*

Tonight let's write down the names of the people we love most in the whole world. Who are some of those people?

*[Let your child write the names on the facing page. If your child is too young to write, write the names as he or she lists them.]*

Now let's use that list as our prayer list. We're going to pray for everyone on that list. I'll start out by praying for the first person; then when I'm finished, you pray for that person, too.

*[Model intercessory prayer by thanking God for each person and for something specific about that person, then asking God to meet that person's needs. Be specific whenever you can. When you and your child have prayed for everyone on the list, close with a blessing prayer like the following.]*

Dear God,
I want to pray for one more person that I love: my dear
_____ *[your child's name].* Thank You for giving us so much love. Bless _____ *[your child's name]* and give him/her a good night's sleep.
     In Jesus' name,
     Amen.

"I thank my God every time I remember you" (Philippians 1:3).

- 

- 

- 

- 

- 

-

### LET'S PRAY FOR OTHERS
# Praying for People We Have a Hard Time Loving

*[You will need a pencil.]*

Tonight let's write down the names of some people who are hard for us to love. Maybe they're people you don't like to play with, or who aren't very kind to you, or that you sometimes fight with. Who are some of those people?

*[Let your child write the names on the facing page. If your child is too young to write, write the names as he or she lists them.]*

Did you know that Jesus wants us to pray for those people? He said, "Love your enemies. Pray for those who hurt you" (Matthew 5:44).

Let's use this list as our prayer list. We're going to pray for everyone on that list. I'll start out by praying for the first person; then when I'm finished, you pray for that person, too.

*[Model intercessory prayer by thanking God for each person and for something specific about that person, then asking God to meet that person's needs. Be specific whenever you can. When you and your child have prayed for everyone on the list, close with a blessing prayer like the following.]*

Dear God,
I want to pray for one more person tonight: my dear
_____ *[your child's name]*. Thank You
that it isn't hard at all for me to love him/her. Bless
_____ *[your child's name]* and give him/her
a good night's sleep.
        In Jesus' name,
        Amen.

- 
- 
- 
- 
- 
-

LET'S DO AN EXPERIMENT
# Paper Airplanes

*[You will need tissues, paper, and waxed paper.]*

Tonight we're going to experiment with paper airplanes. First let's make some predictions.

*[Show your child the tissues, paper, and waxed paper.]*

Which of these do you think will make the best airplane?

How will we decide which airplane is best? Will it be the one that flies the farthest? That we can aim the best? Or what?

*[After you and your child have decided on a criterion for "best airplane," make paper airplanes from a tissue, a piece of paper, and a piece of waxed paper. Then fly them (or try to) to see whether your predictions were correct.]*

Which airplane is the best?

Paper airplanes are supposed to fly, aren't they? If they don't fly, like this one made out of a tissue, they're not doing what they were made for.

Do you know what God made you for?

Listen to this verse from the Bible: "God made us. He created us to belong to Christ Jesus. Now we can do good things. Long ago God prepared them for us to do" (Ephesians 2:10).

God made you to belong to Jesus. Did you know that?

*[If your child has received Jesus as Savior, talk a little about that event. If not, you may want to explain how to begin a relationship with God (see "God So Loved the World," p. 112).]*

And God made you to do good things. What kind of good things do you suppose God wants you to do?

*[Help your child think of specific actions, like obeying parents, sharing with siblings, praying, etc.]*

If you were one of these paper airplanes, would you want to be one that does what it's made for, or one that doesn't?

You're not an airplane; you're a very special child of God. Let's pray that you will always do what God made you for: to belong to Jesus and to do good things.

Dear Jesus,
Thank You for the making _____ *[your child's name]* such a wonderful, special child. Thank You that You love him/her so much that You want him/her to belong to You. Thank You for the good things You planned for _____ *[your child's name]*, like _____ *[list the good actions your child identified].*
　　　Amen.

### LET'S PLANT A SEED
# Light for the Path

*[You will need a flashlight.]*

Let's plant another seed. Not a seed in a pot, but a seed in your heart. Do you remember that Jesus said God's Word is like a seed planted in your heart?

Here is a Bible verse to learn by heart:

"Your word is a lamp to my feet and a light for my path" (Psalm 199:105, NIV).

*[Read the verse and have your child repeat it.]*

Do you know where we can read God's Word? Right here in the Bible.

Let's see if we can figure out what it means that the Bible is like a light for the path.

*[Turn out the room lights.]*

How easy would it be to get from the bed to the bathroom with all the lights out?

What might you bump into on the way?

Do you think you might hurt yourself walking in the dark?

*[Shine the flashlight in a path from the bed to the door.]*

How easy would it be to get from the bed to the bathroom with this flashlight shining on the path?

In the Bible, God doesn't talk about how to get from the bed to the bathroom. But He does tell us how to get from here to heaven. Do you know how?

The Bible tells us that to go to heaven all we have to do is love and trust Jesus and ask Him to forgive our sins. Is that something you've done, or something you can do?

If you can do that, then you know the way to heaven. And the Bible was the light that showed you the way.

Let's read the verse again.

*[Read the verse and have your child repeat it once more.]*

Dear God,
Thank You that _____ _____ *[your child's name]* can have a wonderful future with You in heaven! Thank You for giving us the Bible to show us how we can get there.
        Amen.

### LET'S PLAY A GAME
# Categories

*[You will need a watch with a second hand.]*

This game is a race with words. I'll name a category—like "animals." You see how many things in that category—like cats, dogs, and aardvarks—you can name in one minute while I time you with my watch.

*[As your child lists things, keep track on your fingers. At the end of the minute, announce the total. Then let your child name a category for you. Some easy categories include animals, people's names, colors, food. You can make the categories more challenging by asking for things that begin with a certain letter or that are a certain color. When you're done playing, make comments like the following.]*

What a lot of things we named! And isn't it amazing that God made all those _____ *[name the categories you used; for example, animals, colors, people]*?

Let's thank God for all He made.

Dear God,
What a wonderful, full world You made, full of
_____ *[name the categories you used]*.
Thank You for all You made. Thank You especially for
dear _____ *[your child's name]*.
     Amen.

### LET'S TALK ABOUT THE FUTURE
# A New Room

Do you ever feel ashamed to ask a question because you're afraid it might be "dumb"? There are no stupid questions! Especially when you're talking with God. Here's one written by a seven-year-old named Mark:

Dear Lord,
Will I have my own room in heaven? I am 7 and I sleep in the same room with my brother and two sisters.*

What do you think?

We have an answer in John 14:2 where Jesus said to His disciples: "There are many rooms in my Father's house....I am going there to prepare a place for you."

What would you like your room to be like?

Whatever else heaven is, it is a room in God's house. With Jesus.

Dear Jesus,
Thank You for the room You're getting ready for
_____ [your child's name]. And for my room, too. I hope we're just down the hall from each other. We can't wait to see You.
        Amen.

*From *Dear Lord*, selected by Bill Adler (Thomas Nelson, 1982).

### LET'S DO AN EXPERIMENT
# Taste Test

*[You will need a variety of bite-sized foods, at least one of them sweet. Good choices could include a cracker, a piece of carrot, a bite-sized piece of fruit, and a small candy. Place the foods in a bag so your child can't see them.]*

*[Keep all the foods hidden in the bag.]*

Tonight we're going to do a taste test to see if you can tell what something is just by tasting it. Close your eyes and I will give you a food to taste.

*[One by one, let your child sample each food, guessing what it is after each. End with the sweetest food you have.]*

What was your favorite food?

What was the saltiest?

What was the sweetest?

God tells us that His Word in the Bible is like something sweet to eat—even sweeter than honey!* What do you think that could mean?

It would be good to have some of God's sweet Word every day. When do you think would be a good time to read the Bible together every day?

* Psalm 19:10

*[If you have regular family devotions, affirm that practice. If you don't, think about a time when you could read a Bible verse or Bible story together with your child or as a family. Maybe your child will enjoy thinking of reading the Bible as "dessert" after supper, or as a "sweet" bedtime treat.]*

Dear God,
Thank You for the Bible. Thank You that it is even more wonderful than sweet treats to eat. Please help _____ __ *[your child's name]* to enjoy listening to the Bible—maybe even as much as he/she likes eating _____ *[name a favorite sweet treat]*!
    Amen.

*[Since daily Bible reading is an ongoing discipline, you can use "Honeycomb" on page 186 to reinforce this lesson in a few days or a few weeks.]*

### LET'S PRETEND
# Pig Pens

A long time ago, a 12-year-old girl from Perry County, Alabama, wrote an essay she titled, "True Greatness." Here is how she ended it:

"Once there was a woman that lived near a pig pen, & when the wind blew that way it was very smelly, & at first when she went there she could not smell anything but pig, but when she lived there for a while, she learned to smell the clover blossoms thru it. That was true greatness."

Do you think you'd rather smell a pig pen, or clover flowers?

Let's pretend that the things we don't like about people smell like pig pens. And let's pretend the things we like about people smell like flowers.

Tell me the name of someone who bugs you sometimes. Why does that person bug you?

*[Make a mental note of the details your child shares.]*

Close your eyes and let's take a pretend smelling tour.

*[Have your child close his or her eyes while you narrate the following "tour."]*

Hmm, who's that I see? I think it's _____
*[name the person your child mentioned]*.

Uh-oh! I smell _____ *[name the
things your child dislikes about this person]*.

I don't want to smell that, so I'm going to find some
flowers to smell. I think I'll smell _____
*[name some specific positive things about the person]*.

OK, you can open your eyes.

When you are with _____ *[the person
your child mentioned]*, do you usually try to smell the pig
pen or the flowers? I mean, do you think all the time
about what bugs you, or do you try to find the good
things about this person?

Let's ask God to help us smell the flowers and not the
pig pen.

Dear God,
Help us to be like that woman who lived near the pig pen.
Help us not to think so much about what bugs us about
people. Help us instead to find the good things about
them. Especially help _____ *[your child's
name]* find the good things about _____ *[the
person your child mentioned]*. And thank You, God, that to
me _____ *[your child's name]* is the sweetest
flower there could be!
　　　Amen.

LET'S TALK ABOUT FEELINGS
# Scabs

*[You will need several adhesive bundages.]*

Why do you think we get a scab when we skin some part of our body?

A scab is sort of like a natural bandage. When you get cut, healthy cells come to help those that got scraped. They make a scab to keep the blood in and the germs out.

*[Show your child the adhesive bandages.]*

These bandages are like artificial scabs. They keep the blood in and the germs out, too. Do you have any scrapes that need a bandage?

*[If your child does, put a bandage on the sore.]*

Sometimes we get hurt on the inside, too, don't we? Our feelings get hurt. People can't see that the way they can

See a cut or scrape, but hurt feelings are just as real as hurt knees or elbows. And they hurt just as bad. Sometimes worse.

Do you have any hurt feelings inside? Tell me about them.

I would like to put a bandage on your hurt feelings and make them all better.

*[Put an imaginary bandage over your child's heart.]*

But do you know who can really make your hurt feelings better? Jesus. Let's ask Him to do that.

Dear Jesus,

_____'s *[your child's name]* feelings are hurt about _____ *[name the hurt feelings your child identified]*. I love _____ *[your child's name]* very much, and I would like him/her not to feel hurt inside. Will You please help heal those hurt feelings, just as You help _____'s *[your child's name]* scrapes and cuts to heal? Thank You.

    Amen.

### LET'S LOOK AT NATURE
# Honeycomb

*[You will need a piece of bread, a knife, and a jar of honey that has honeycomb in it.]*

*[Use this as a follow-up several days or weeks after "Taste Test" (p. 180).]*

Look in this jar of honey. Do you know what is in it?

The odd-looking thing you see in the honey is the honeycomb. It's part of how bees make honey.

When bees go out into the fields, they gather nectar from the flowers. Nectar is kind of a sugary juice that is stored in flowers. The bees take the nectar back to the hive, add certain chemicals from their bodies called enzymes, and put the mixture in the honeycombs. Then, special bees in the hive fan the nectar with their wings. The fanning, along with the heat inside the hive, makes the water in the nectar dry up. What's left behind is honey!

Would you like to taste it?

*[Open jar and put a little on a piece of bread for your child to sample.]*

Do you remember that the Bible says God's Word is "sweeter than honey that is taken from the honeycomb"

(Psalm 19:10a)? What has God taught you from the
Bible that is special?

Dear Lord,
We thank You for Your word in the Bible, which in a way
is like this honeycomb, dripping with sweet and satisfy-
ing goodness. Yum! Thank You for giving us a taste.
Keep blessing _____ *[your child's name]*
every time he/she hears the Bible.

     Amen.

## LET'S DO AN EXPERIMENT
# Floating Finger

*[Practice this first, so that you can help your child see the optical illusion. Hold your hands about 15 inches in front of you at eye level with your index fingers about an inch apart. Don't look at your fingers; instead focus on something a few feet beyond your fingers. Slowly move your fingers closer to your eyes, still focusing on the object a few feet away. A "floating finger" will appear in the air between your fingers.]*

Tonight we're going to find a floating finger.

*[Help your child position his or her fingers. Identify an object beyond his or her fingers for your child to focus on. Then have your child move his or her fingers until the "floating finger" appears.]*

What do you see?

Now change your focus to look *at* your fingers instead of past them. What happens now?

Is there really a floating finger somewhere in this room?

If we believed that floating finger we saw was real, that would be pretty silly, wouldn't it? But sometimes people do believe in things that aren't real. Can you think of any examples?

*[Use this time to talk about things that
are issues to your child, whether it's
believing real people can do the
things shown in the cartoons, or
fear of imaginary monsters, or tall
tales they hear from their friends,
or a fable like Santa Claus
or the Easter Bunny
that you don't want
them to accept.]*

Sometimes it can be
hard to know what's
real and what isn't. But
one thing we can
always know is real:
God's love. Let's thank Him for that.

Dear God,
Help us to realize that not everything we see or think we
see is real. Help _____ _____ *[your child's name]*
with _____ *[identify any fears or misconcep-
tions you discussed with your child]*. Thank You that
You are real. And thank You that Your love for
_____ *[your child's name]* is very, very real!
    Amen.

### LET'S DO AN EXPERIMENT
# Ticklish Toes

Let's see your feet. Hand them over. Or should I say, feet them over!

*[Once you have your child's feet in your hands, begin tickling them. If your child has a condition that prevents you from tickling his or her feet, tickle a different part of the body.]*

Have you ever wondered why feet are so ticklish?

Nerve endings make the skin feel what's touching it. The more nerve endings, the more that part of the body feels—and the more ticklish it is!

Let's make some predictions.

Do you think your ears are more or less ticklish than your feet? Let's find out.

*[Tickle the ears.]*

Do you think the ears have more nerve endings than the feet or fewer?

What do you predict about your arms? Will they be more or less ticklish?

*[Tickle the arms.]*

What about your ribs?

*[Tickle the ribs.]*

Of all those places, which was the most ticklish?

For most people, the most nerve endings are in the feet. And that is why feet are so much fun!

*[Grab your child's feet and tickle them again.]*

Dear God,
We thank You for skin and for the nerve endings that let us feel. Thank You for tickles! And thank You for this wonderful child to tickle!
     Amen.

### LET'S TALK ABOUT FEELINGS
## Popping with Anger

*[You will need some popcorn in a bowl.]*

*[Allow your child to help you pop some popcorn before bedtime and take a bowl into the bedroom. Enjoy the popcorn together.]*

Let's see if we can find a kernel that didn't pop.

*[Find an unpopped or partially popped kernel and look at it.]*

How do you think the popcorn gets out of the kernel?

Here's how. Every kernel of corn has a tiny droplet of water in it. When you heat the kernel, the water turns to steam. And since steam expands, taking up more space than water, it presses against the walls of the kernel until it explodes.

We're all a little like that kernel of popcorn when we get angry. A little bit of anger can get bigger and bigger until suddenly our anger explodes out in yelling or crying or a tantrum.

Have you ever felt like you had anger ready to explode inside you? Tell me about it. What is it that steamed you up?

Let's see what the Bible has to say about anger: "Everyone ... should be slow to get angry. A man's anger doesn't produce the kind of life God wants" (James 1:19b-20).

How do you think I can help you slow down your anger so it doesn't explode?

*[Talk with your child about a specific situation in which he or she has trouble controlling his or her temper. Together come up with possible solutions such as leaving the room, counting to 20, asking for a hug.]*

Let's ask God to help keep our anger from exploding, too.

Dear God,
We like it when popcorn explodes. But we don't like it when our anger explodes. Please help me not to explode at _____ *[your child's name]*. And help _____ *[your child's name]* to try _____ *[list the possible solutions you discussed]* next time he/she feels anger heating up inside. Thank You that You don't stay angry with us! *
    Amen.

* Psalm 103:8-9

LET'S PRETEND
# Mirrors

Let's look at each other and pretend we're looking in a mirror. You be the person looking in the mirror, and I'll be the mirror.

Here are the rules. The mirror has to do everything the person looking in the mirror does. But the mirror can't laugh—unless the person who's looking in the mirror laughs. If the mirror laughs, you have to change places.

*[Let your child make faces and move around, while you mime every move. If you laugh, switch places. Even if you don't, trade places after a while. You can do things like pretending to put on make-up, checking your teeth, flapping your ears and pretending you're flying, combing your hair, showing off your muscles, pretending you're carrying on a conversation with someone.]*

Was it easy or hard to follow my example when you were the mirror?

What was the most fun example to follow?

Paul wrote a letter to Christians talking about following an example. Here's what he wrote: "Follow my example, just as I follow the example of Christ" (1 Corinthians 11:1).

Paul wasn't talking about pretending to be mirrors. He was talking about watching and following the example of how Christians should live.

What Christians do you know who set a good example for you to follow?

*[Briefly talk with your child about a specific Christian role model and what your child can learn from that person. Focus on concrete actions that your child has observed, such as the way an older woman at church remembers to send birthday cards, or the way the pastor prays for the sick.]*

Let's talk to God about this.

Dear God,
Thank You for _____ *[the role model you discussed]* and the way he/she follows Jesus' example by _____ *[name a specific action]*. Help _____ *[your child's name]* to follow his/her example. And help _____ *[your child's name]* to be a good example, too, especially to younger children who look up to him/her.
     Amen.

## LET'S WRITE A POEM
# Name Acrostic

*[You will need a pencil and paper.]*

Let's write a poem. Some poems rhyme, but not all poems do. Some poems start each line with a certain letter. Some poems in the Bible start each line with a different letter of the Hebrew alphabet.

In our poem, each line is going to start with a letter of your name.

*[Write your child's name vertically on a piece of paper.]*

Let's think of something you like about yourself that starts with the first letter of your name. It could be one word or lots of words.

*[Help your child think of words and fill in the acrostic. Don't worry about making the lines similar to each other—this poem is about process, not product! Be sure to add your own suggestions of your child's positive qualities. Here's an example to spark your thinking:*

> *P retty good at soccer*
> *E xcited about Taylor's birthday party*
> *T all*
> *E ating pizza is something he likes*
> *R uns really fast]*

*[When you're done, read the poem aloud, then move into a prayer like the following.]*

Dear God,
You have made _____ *[your child's name]*
such a special person. Thank You for _____
*[list the positive qualities from the poem].* And thank You
for giving him/her to me to love!
     Amen.

### LET'S TELL A STORY
## Once Upon a Time...

Tonight let's tell a story. Or maybe two or three. Here's how we're going to do it. One of us will start a make-believe story. I'll go first. And then after a while, I'll point to you, and you pick up where I left off, making it as wild and crazy a story as you want. Then after a while, you point to me, and I'll pick up the story. And we'll go back and forth until the person who started the story wants to end it. Sound like fun? I'll start.

Once upon a time . . .

*[Let the story go as long as you like. If you get stuck, try throwing in one of these lines:*

- *Then suddenly an enormous T. Rex came thundering along, charging straight at...*

- *All at once, a beautiful fairy princess appeared. She waved her wand and said...*

- *Without warning, a huge hole opened up and swallowed...*

- *Unexpectedly, _____'s [the main character] nose turned to cheese...*

*If you are stuck for an ending, this one always works:*

• *Then _____ (your child's name) woke up and discovered it had all been a dream.]*

Dear God,
Thank You for stories and for the fun we have not only in telling them but in listening, too. Thank You for telling us the wonderful and exciting stories in the Bible. Some of them sound almost too amazing to be true, but we know they are.
Give _____ [your child's name] a good night's sleep. And may his/her dreams be good ones. In Jesus' name we pray.
      Amen.

### LET'S HEAR A STORY
# Guardian Angels

*[This story is a paraphrase of Matthew 18:1-11.]*

God loves children very much. A story in the Bible shows us how much God loves children just like you.

Once Jesus' followers wanted to know who would be the most important person in God's kingdom. Probably they were all hoping that Jesus would say, "Why, you'll be the most important, of course!"

But Jesus didn't say that. Instead, Jesus called a little child to come over to Him. Now, you know how sometimes some grown-ups think that children can't be important until they get bigger. Maybe Jesus' followers were thinking that, too.

So they were probably pretty surprised to hear Jesus say, "Do you want to know who is important to Me? Look at this child. Little children are so important that God the Father has put an angel in charge of watching over each one. And every angel that watches over a child can go talk to God the Father in heaven any time."

That's how important children are to God!

That's how important you are to God!

Dear God,
Thank You that _____ *[your child's name]* is so important to You that You put an angel in charge of watching over him/her. Thank You that even when I can't be there to watch and protect _____ *[your child's name],* an angel is watching out for him/her. Thank You for how precious this child is to You. And how precious he/she is to me, too.
    Amen.

LET'S LOOK IN THE BIBLE
## Jesus Is the Way

*[You will need a Bible.]*

Let's listen in on a conversation Jesus had with His disciples shortly before He went home to be with His Father in heaven.

*[Read John 14:1-6.]*

What do you think Jesus meant when He said He was the Way? The way where?

When Jesus died on the cross, He made a way for us that stretched from earth to heaven—kind of like an escalator.

Have you ever ridden an escalator?

To get from the lower floor to the upper floor, do you have to have superhuman powers to jump that high?

Do you have to climb the walls with your bare hands?

Do you have to build an escalator yourself?

No. That's already been done for you. What do you have to do? Just take one step, that's all, and the escalator will take you there.

That one step is what the Bible calls the step of faith. Faith means believing that God will forgive your sins and help you always be close to Him—right now and after you die.

Jesus is like the escalator to God. All it takes to get there is one step. *[If your child has already taken this step, affirm that. If not, you could ask the following question.]* Would you like to take that step tonight, or is it something you want to think about for a while?

*[If your child wishes to take that step of faith, guide him or her in a prayer like this: "Dear Jesus, I know that I disobey You. I am sorry for all the wrong things I do. Please forgive me. I want to be close to You and to God the Father. Amen."]*

Dear Jesus,
Thank You that You are the Way to be close to God. Thank You that we don't have to make our own way to God. Thank You that You did everything we need to be close to God when You died on the cross. Please help
_____ *[your child's name]* always to love and be close to You.
        Amen.

# Answer Pages

### Page 26—"Puppy Puzzle"

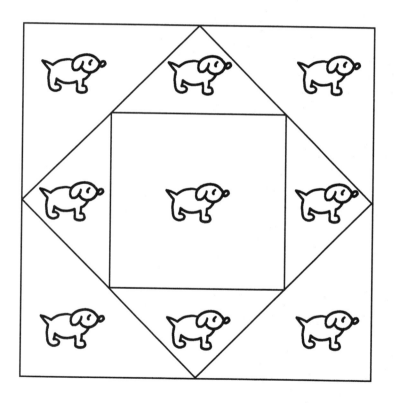

**Page 62—"Squares, Squares Everywhere"**
There are 30 squares.

**Page 70—"Toothpick Teaser"**
Break one of the toothpicks in half and place the two
pieces at right angles to the others.

**Page 76—"Little Riddles"**
1. A towel.
2. You threw the baseball straight up.
3. Jane can reach the first floor button on the elevator,
   but is too short to reach the tenth floor button. She
   can reach the button for the seventh floor, though.

**Page 92—"At the Zoo"**

It was a bad day at the zoo.
The weasels got the measles.
The gnu got the flu
The crickets got rickets.
The fox got the pox.
The mice got lice.
The beavers got fevers.
The snakes got the shakes.

**Page 104—"Mystery Doodles"**

1. Sun rising over a rocket ship
2. Eyeglasses for a Cyclops
3. A snake underwater

# *Welcome to the Family!*

Heritage
Builders

*Helping You Build a Family of Faith*

We hope you've enjoyed this book. Heritage Builders was founded in 1995 by three fathers with a passion for the next generation. As a new ministry of Focus on the Family, Heritage Builders strives to equip, train and motivate parents to become intentional about building a strong spiritual heritage.

It's quite a challenge for busy parents to find ways to build a spiritual foundation for their families—especially in a way they enjoy and understand. Through activities and participation, children can learn biblical truth in a way they can understand, enjoy—and *remember.*

Passing along a heritage of Christian faith to your family is a parent's highest calling. Heritage Builders' goal is to encourage and empower you in this great mission with practical resources and inspiring ideas that really work—and help your children develop a lasting love for God.

\*\*\*

## *How To Reach Us*

For more information, visit our Heritage Builders Web site! Log on to **www.heritagebuilders.com** to discover new resources, sample activities, and ideas to help you pass on a spiritual heritage. To request any of these resources, simply call Focus on the Family at 1-800-A-FAMILY (1-800-232-6459) or in Canada, call 1-800-661-9800. Or send your request to Focus on the Family, Colorado Springs, CO 80995. In Canada, write Focus on the Family, P.O. Box 9800, Stn. Terminal, Vancouver, B.C. V6B 4G3

To learn more about Focus on the Family or to find out if there is an associate office in your country, please visit www. family.org

We'd love to hear from you!

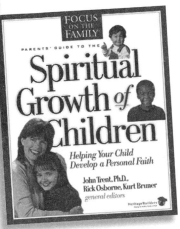

## Mealtime Moments

Make your family's time around the dinner table meaningful with *Mealtime Moments,* a book that brings you great discussion starters and activities for teaching your children about your faith. Kids will have fun getting involved with games, trivia questions and theme nights, all based on spiritually sound ideas. Perfect for the whole family! Spiralbound.

## Joy Ride!

Use your drive time to teach your kids how faith can be part of everyday life with *Joy Ride!* A wonderful resource for parents, this book features activities, puzzles, games and discussion starters to help get your kids thinking about—and living out—what they believe.

• • •

Visit our Heritage Builders Web site! Log on to **www.heritagebuilders.com** to discover new resources, sample activities, and ideas to help you pass on a spiritual heritage. To request any of these resources, simply call Focus on the Family at 1-800-A-FAMILY (1-800-232-6459) or in Canada, call 1-800-661-9800. Or send your request to Focus on the Family, Colorado Springs, CO 80995. In Canada, write Focus on the Family, P.O. Box 9800, Stn. Terminal, Vancouver, B.C. V6B 4G3.

Heritage Builders

*Helping You Build a Family of Faith*

Every family has a heritage—a spiritual, emotional, and social legacy passed from one generation to the next. There are four main areas we at Heritage Builders recommend parents consider as they plan to pass their faith to their children:

### Family Fragrance

Every family's home has a fragrance. Heritage Builders encourages parents to create a home environment that fosters a sweet, Christ-centered AROMA of love through Affection, Respect, Order, Merriment, and Affirmation.

### Family Traditions

Whether you pass down stories, beliefs and/or customs, traditions can help you establish a special identity for your family. Heritage Builders encourages parents to set special "milestones" for their children to help guide them and move them through their spiritual development.

### Family Compass

Parents have the unique task of setting standards for normal, healthy living through their attitudes, actions and beliefs. Heritage Builders encourages parents to give their children the moral navigation tools they need to succeed on the roads of life.

### Family Moments

Creating special, teachable moments with their children is one of a parent's most precious and sometimes, most difficult responsibilities. Heritage Builders encourages parents to capture little moments throughout the day to teach and impress values, beliefs, and biblical principles onto their children.

We look forward to standing alongside you as you seek to impart the Lord's care and wisdom onto the next generation—onto your children.

Heritage Builders

*Helping You Build a Family of Faith*